RELEASED

The
Working Class
in Modern
Europe

PROBLEMS IN
EUROPEAN CIVILIZATION

Under the editorial direction of
John Ratté
Amherst College

The
Working Class
in Modern
Europe

Edited and with an introduction by

Mary Lynn McDougall

Smith College

D. C. HEATH AND COMPANY
Lexington, Massachusetts   Toronto   London

CONTENTS

INTRODUCTION

Until the end of the nineteenth century, workers rarely appeared in historical writing. When they did appear, it was usually in the guise of the faceless "rabble" or "mob." The very terms aroused fear and repugnance in the "respectable" reader, and in case the terms alone did not produce this effect, conservative historians such as Hippolyte Taine went on to define them as the "many-headed brute" or the "band of savages."[1] Beginning in the 1840s, republican historians like Jules Michelet introduced the no less faceless but considerably less fearsome "crowd" or "people." About the same time, early Socialist and Communist theorists—Blanc, Marx, Proudhon—were popularizing the terms "proletariat" and "working class." For these social theorists, the words had a positive denotation; for many of their readers they had negative connotations. Either way, though, the ideas were abstract. Very few *engagé* Socialists actually attempted to portray individual workers, and even then these workers were singled out only because they were important political activists.

In the last decade of the nineteenth century, the working class began to figure prominently in certain historical studies. A completely new field of history developed: the field of labor history. This development was tied to the advent of large Socialist parties. In Britain two Fabian Socialists, Sydney and Beatrice Webb, wrote their *History of Trade Unionism;* in France the Socialist Emile Levasseur published his history of the working class and industry in France; in Germany the Social Democrat Franz Mehring put out the standard history of the Social Democratic party. Later the Hammonds, Mark Hovell, G. D. H. Cole and Raymond Postgate expanded on the work

---

[1] *The French Revolution* (New York, 1878), vol. I, pp. 66, 67.

of the Webbs; E. Martin Saint-Léon, Pierre Louis, Georges Duveau and Jean Bruhat carried on the work begun by Levasseur. German labor historians tended to confine themselves to histories of the Social Democratic or Communist parties, but the East German Communist, Jurgen Kuczynski, like his French contemporary, Eduard Dolléans, even extended his work beyond his native country to the whole of Western Europe.[2]

Over a half-century, the labor historians accomplished a great deal. Labor history was accepted as a legitimate (if not quite genteel) field of scholarly inquiry. The working class was shown to be an important force in modern European history, and more significantly (since the workers' impact on certain periods could hardly be ignored), workers were portrayed as capable of independent, rational and positive action. The labor historians did not just introduce the "working class" into historical studies; they introduced them *sympathetically*. In so doing, they opened new areas of research, discovered new sources of information and new ways of using old sources.

Along with their numerous accomplishments, the early labor historians had certain limitations. Because all of them were connected directly or indirectly with the Labor, Social Democratic or Communist party of their respective countries, each tended to focus upon those aspects of labor history that contributed to the development of his party and related institutions such as trade unions. Their focus was not dictated by their parties, for few submitted their work to their parties for approval. Rather, their subject matter was determined by their interest in the growth of their parties, and more generally in the movements to which they belonged. The crucial point is that they either ignored or paid scant attention to whole areas of what can rightfully be considered labor history, even given the most narrow interpretation, that is, a history of the labor movement.

For example, virtually all of the early labor historians omitted or passed quickly over those elements of worker activism that did not foreshadow or add to the labor movement as it appeared in the last two decades of the nineteenth century. Archaic or unacceptable forms of worker protest and organization were rarely discussed. When they were, it was with little empathy and sometimes with con-

---

[2] For more complete bibliographical information, see the Suggestions for Additional Reading at the end of this book.

descension. As the most telling critic of the first generation of labor historians expressed it, they were writing about the winners, not the losers, in the labor movement.[3]

Related to this omission, but going beyond it in scope, was the early labor historians' preoccupation with institutions or organizations. To read many of their histories is to read about the infrastructure and in-fighting of one association or committee, one federation or congress, after the other. The difficulty with this kind of history (other than the confusion it can cause) is that it excludes working-class protests such as machine-breaking, early strikes, street demonstrations and insurrections, which were not institutionalized or organized in very explicit ways. More important, this kind of history excludes consideration of the workers other than the outstanding working-class leaders, whether these workers participated in the movement, or, especially, if they did not. These histories were definitely not concerned with the apathetic worker.

Part of the problem stemmed from the early labor historian's interest in the development of national and international labor movements. The chronological format and the national or international focus precluded in-depth analysis, particularly at a local level.[4] This lack of analysis did not affect the study of labor organizations as much as it did the study of the people who made up the organizations—and the people who did not belong to any organization. Few of the first generation of labor historians went beyond the classic economic explanation of labor militancy to the broader social preconditions for militancy or nonmilitancy. Only Georges Duveau and the Hammonds made a real effort to carry the search for the intellectual roots of militancy beyond the ideas of predominantly bourgeois Socialists and Communists, into the minds or mentality of the workers themselves. Duveau and the Hammonds also stood alone in their broader concern with the workers' society and culture. Generally speaking, the older labor historians were not open to the methods being developed in other social sciences.

By the late 1940s and early 1950s, a new generation of labor historians entered the field. While this new generation respected the accomplishments of their predecessors, they were also critical

---

[3] E. P. Thompson, *The Making of the English Working Class* (New York, 1963), p. 12.
[4] G. Rudé, *Debate on Europe* (New York, 1972), pp. 187–188.

of their limitations. More positively, these historians tried to fill in the gaps and expand the field. Although many of them were affiliated with the Labor, Socialist or Communist parties of the period—and still more considered themselves Marxists—they were not solely or even primarily interested in the growth of their parties and organized labor. Historians like E. J. Hobsbawm, E. P. Thompson and George Rudé wrote about archaic forms of worker protest, trying to prove that these types of protest had rational goals, informal organization and, occasionally, some short-term success. They did so by studying the workers who participated in these actions. They carefully analyzed the local political, economic and social contexts in which the actions occurred, and Hobsbawm and Rudé also drew comparisons between local conditions across national borders. Most important, all three tried to reconstruct the protestors' perceptions of their context and their reasons for protesting. E. P. Thompson summed up their efforts as an attempt to view history "from below."[5]

Hobsbawm, Thompson and Rudé were all undogmatic Marxists. Consequently there is little resemblance between their work and the stereotype of Marxist history. Indeed, the aspect of their work that has attracted the most attention is their innovative methodology. If Eric Hobsbawm continued to give great weight to long-term, structural changes in the economy as a factor producing militancy, he did not confine himself to such an explanation. Instead he went on to the broader institutional context of militancy. Along the same lines, he employed statistical evidence but warned of the inadequacy of the fragmentary and gross statistics of the past. Here he was surpassed by Edward Thompson, who doubted whether the most complete and accurate statistics could tell us what is important about working-class life. Thompson drew on a wide variety of impressionistic source materials, including police and judicial records, to recreate the working-class society, culture, mentality and politics. Rudé tended to rely more exclusively on police and judicial records to analyze the composition and expectations of worker crowds.

These three Marxists are probably the most widely known of the new generation of labor historians, but there are many non-Marxists who have brought fresh methods and insights to the writing of working-class history. In some respects, the non-Marxists have more

[5] E. P. Thompson, "History from Below," *Times* (London) *Literary Supplement,* April 7, 1966, pp. 279–280.

seriously questioned the old orthodoxies. Asa Briggs, who has contributed to so many fields of history, has performed a valuable service in encouraging local studies and using them to point out the deep-seated divisions within the national Chartist movement. An American scholar, Peter N. Stearns, has compiled data on long periods of strike activity, analyzed these data and used the results to question some of the earlier, more ideological interpretations of strike activity. In his study of the German Social Democratic party, Guenther Roth used a sociological approach to show how the party became a "state within a state." Perhaps his most interesting findings were those concerning what Marxism and the party meant to the average working-class member. James Joll, whose brilliant work on anarchists follows the more traditional pattern of a study of leaders, their ideas and actions, nevertheless indicates how working-class "syndicalists" (unionists) were able to persuade the more bourgeois leadership.

While most working-class histories still focus on "the movement," there have been some notable exceptions. The debate on the standard of living of workers during the Industrial Revolution has been the most famous (or infamous, given the sharpness of the attacks in this most ideological exchange). This debate has been the subject of another book in the Problems in European Civilization Series.[6] But the topic has not been exhausted—and not only because the ideological undertones and statistical problems seem unavoidable. Rather, whole areas of research have been ignored in the constant concern with wage, price, consumption and mortality figures. The problem of working-class housing, a major problem, has only recently been explored by historians like Anthony Wohl. The effect of industrialization and urbanization on the working-class family only began to be studied systematically in the 1950s, when the sociologists Michael Young and Peter Willmott examined contemporary kinship patterns in a London working-class district. Now Michael Anderson has employed some of their concepts, as well as his own very sophisticated statistical methods, to reveal an unexpected strength in the working-class family in a typical industrial town in Lancashire during the nineteenth century. Other historians have begun to ex-

[6] P. A. M. Taylor, *The Industrial Revolution in Britain: Triumph or Disaster?* (rev. ed.; Lexington, Mass., 1970).

amine the assumptions about working-class sexuality. A few highly articulate "veterans" of working-class ghettos—children of workers who managed to get a higher education and leave those ghettos— have written memoirs that vividly recreate the society of the ghetto and call into question some of the accepted interpretations of it.

In the past twenty-five years, the new labor historians have produced much fine work and upset many complacent opinions. As yet they have not offered a comprehensive view of modern European labor history. The coincidence of the rich variety of the new labor history and the lack of an overall framework makes it difficult to choose a limited number of examples. The selections collected here were made on the basis of four principles: (1) that each of the three main areas of research be included; (2) that within each of these categories, some of the outstanding events and issues be discussed; (3) that different approaches appear; and (4) that the major new labor historians and some of their interesting younger colleagues be represented. Important omissions are inevitable and unavoidable. Wherever possible, the omissions will be noted and the relevant source indicated. Where more work might be done—and there is much work to be done—that too will be mentioned.

The principles of selection require some elaboration. The first one, that the three main areas of research be included, has informed the division of the text into three units: on economic activism, political militancy, and working-class life. However, the units are not necessarily mutually exclusive. Some selections subsumed under the heading economic activism discuss organizations and actions that have a basic economic motive, but also have political overtones. Similarly, some contributions on political militancy mention economic factors. Contributions to both of the units on "the movement" connect whatever aspect of the movement they are studying to general economic, political or social developments. On the other hand, the sociologists and historians represented in the unit on working-class life tend not to deal with the movement.

These sociologists and historians are not alone; most scholars who study working-class life avoid the movement. The reason is understandable: so little work has been done on working-class life that they have had to confine themselves to it alone. The results of their work have substantially altered our conception of working-class life, except as it interacts with the movement. The only authors interested primarily in working-class society and culture who have addressed themselves to this interaction have been workers or former workers. These authors are usually too *engagé;* they exaggerate the importance of the movement. Others, like Robert Roberts in the last selection, seem to be hostile witnesses. (But Roberts's idea that intra-class divisions were more significant than class consciousness is a good antidote to the facile assumptions of universal class consciousness.) As a result, there is a need for dispassionate studies of the whole range of working-class life, a part of which is activism. At present these studies will have to be local in scope; later the results can be correlated and the outline of the broader working-class experience be revealed.

The second principle of selection—that some of the outstanding events and issues be discussed—also calls for elucidation. In many ways the French Revolution was a starting point for modern labor history. Unfortunately its long-term impact on the labor movement and on workers in general has more often been assumed than examined carefully. For this reason it is assumed here, not examined. Other "milestones" are omitted. Instead, the emphasis has been on typical methods of organizing and acting over the century and a half since the French Revolution. In the section on economic activism this means a focus on primitive industrial protest, early strike patterns, transitional unions, and modern strike activity. The section on political militancy includes work on early political organization, the "crowd," a turn-of-the-century Socialist party, a twentieth-century anarchist group and a Labor party in and out of power. But it is the unit on working-class life that best illustrates the stress on issues, for here housing, the family, sexuality, morality and communities are discussed.

The last two principles of selection (diversity of approach and representation of the most interesting "new" labor historians) need little comment. With the exception of the first two selections, there has been no attempt to present contrasting interpretations of the same phenomenon. Moreover, almost all of the contributors attempt to view history "from below." Nevertheless, the contributors do give different weights to different factors. For example, E. P. Thompson is inclined to give an important role to radical political ideologies in economic activism; Peter N. Stearns is not. Arthur Mitzman credits the 1936 and 1937 sit-in strikers in France with important political concerns, but denies that the Communist party molded these concerns. The examples could be multiplied. The only serious divergence that may not be readily apparent can be discerned in Thompson's belief that a single working class emerged in England after 1832 and took political form in the Chartist agitation, and Briggs's belief that divisions within the working class continued to be significant after 1832, especially among the Chartists. In this case the contrast may be explained by Thompson's national purview and loose definition of class, versus the local focus and stricter definition of class that Briggs uses.

Thompson's and Briggs's differences over the definition of class raises a question of overriding importance to this book: what is meant by working class? As all the selections on the early period of the movement will indicate, the early movement was not one of the industrial proletariat. Rather it was composed of artisans, some of them independent masters, more of them dependent masters, and many, journeymen. The independent masters cannot even be considered wage laborers, although the dependent masters' and the journeymen's piece-rates were, in effect, wages. Nor were all of the workers in Robert Roberts's slum "conscious" of themselves as members of a class in opposition to another class. Thus neither the older, simpler concept of the working class as the industrial proletariat, nor the newer, more sophisticated version of a class conscious of itself and its opposition to another class, can cover the phenomena described hereafter. Instead the term working class has been used in its broadest, most flexible sense, to mean all those who have had to do physical labor to earn a living.

Each unit and each selection poses particular problems. The unit on economic activism not only introduces types of economic organization; it poses problems about their causes and their relationships with other organizations. The unit begins, appropriately enough, with an excerpt from E. P. Thompson's *The Making of the English Working Class.* In the excerpt, Thompson criticizes the Hammonds and other early labor historians for seeing Luddism (early nineteenth-century machine-breaking) as a purely industrial activity, and not seeing its political, indeed revolutionary, aims. He uses the same sources as the earlier historians, but refuses to accept their interpretation that widespread reports of revolutionary schemes can be attributed solely to *agents-provocateurs.*

It is precisely this emphasis on the more primitive types of activism and the propensity to see political goals in them that has aroused Thompson's critics most. Many of their criticisms have been as speculative as they claim Thompson's arguments to be. Now, though, there is a good study, based on solid, specific research, that questions one of Thompson's links between the Luddites and the constitutional reformers. A section of this study by Roy Church and S. D. Chapman appears as the second selection. The study carefully considers a single but important constitutional reformer's attitude toward Luddism. Much more of this very precise research, particularly on less prominent working-class leaders, remains to be done.

In the third selection, Professor Stearns explains the lack of industrial strike activity in France during the 1830s and 1840s by reference to governmental and industrial repression, economic insecurity and fears, and social and psychological disorientation. He goes on to attribute what strike activity there was to particularly well-paid male artisans, working in prosperous industries and accustomed to their surroundings. This dual approach—asking why some workers did not strike while others did—has rarely been pursued so methodically, nor produced such interesting results. Professor Stearns's suggestions about the negative effects of immigration and the positive effects of a pre-existent working-class community on worker activism, deserve more attention, especially in more local contexts. Work on early economic and political activism in Marseilles and Toulon (not reproduced here) has modified the purely negative view of immigration by showing that immigrants can also be most open to new ideas—and most in need of change. By contrast, a study of the glassmakers of Carmaux insists on the necessity of immigrants settling down before they could organize and act effectively.

Other scholars make other correlations. Professor Hobsbawm's work on general labor unions in Britain, part of which forms the fourth selection, suggests that these unions arose and developed in the way they did because of a number of economic, social and political factors: the level of industrialization, especially in certain industries; the rhythm of the business cycle; the willingness of employers to negotiate; the amount of social tension; and the presence of Socialists. The fifth selection, derived from an article by Arthur Mitzman on the French sit-in strikes of 1936 and 1937, indicates that strikes could have important political motivations and consequences in the period when the Socialists first came to power. (The French sit-in strikes of 1968 and the British coal miners' strike of 1974 prove that widespread or crucial strikes continue to have political implications.)

The unit on political militancy is also eclectic, for the contributors are not solely concerned with describing political behavior. Professor Briggs's excerpt explains the difference between the "physical-force" Chartists and the "moral-force" Chartists in terms of different geographic and professional constituencies. The physical-force men were centered in the north and drew support from the despairing textile workers; the moral-force men came from the south and recruited among the relatively prosperous artisans. George Rudé's article analyzes who—what professional categories—joined the crowd in the French Revolution of 1848 and why they did. Professor Roth's contribution underscores the role of German Social Democracy as a subculture, a whole way of life that satisfied worker resentments and desires, particularly their desire to belong to and to participate in collective action. James Joll shows how the anarchists who directed their attention to political leaders learned from the syndicalists to emphasize economic activism. The final article in this unit, by W. Campbell-Balfour, deals with the labor movement in Britain during the depression of the 1930s, and so can hardly avoid the degree to which economic and political actions overlapped.

The selections in the last unit either challenge older interpretations of aspects of working-class life, or offer new interpretations of previously unstudied aspects of that life. Anthony S. Wohl's excerpt on working-class housing in nineteenth-century London points out the critical problem of overcrowding and the way in which legislation and institutions designed to mitigate its effects actually intensified the problem. Michael Anderson's contribution on the working-class family in a new industrial town during the Industrial Revolution seriously undermines earlier assumptions that the worker's family disintegrated under the impact of industrialization, by proving that many families had to stick together in order to cope with recurring crises in an age lacking bureaucratized forms of assistance. Michael Young and Peter Willmott, on the other hand, show that the resulting form of working-class kinship in Britain, based on daily contacts between mothers and their married daughters, began to break down when families moved to housing estates in the suburbs. In a pioneering article, part of which is reproduced here, Robert P. Neumann looks at lower-class sexuality and morality in Imperial Germany and concludes that urban workers were not as "immoral" by comparison to agricultural laborers as is often suggested. Furthermore, he doubts whether the decline in traditional morality can be attributed to industrialization alone. Finally, a highly articulate product of a working-class slum, Robert Roberts, examines the slum he grew up in and underlines its rigid caste structure and morality.

Other more specific issues are raised by these selections, and they are left to the introductory remarks preceding each selection.

I ECONOMIC ACTIVISM, 1811-1937

E. P. Thompson

LUDDISM, A REVOLUTIONARY MOVEMENT

Edward Palmer Thompson has been a lecturer at the universities of Leeds and Warwick, as well as the chairman of the board of editors of the New Left Review. *He writes about workers with an empathy born of a humane mind and a committed political position. In his major work,* The Making of the English Working Class *(1963), Thompson deals with the social, psychological and political impact of the Industrial Revolution on British workers, as well as the more usual economic consequences. Moreover, he examines the effect of other factors on working-class culture and politics, and particularly the effect of governmental policies on working-class politics. His interpretations are often unique, and therefore controversial. The interpretation that has aroused the most objections is his emphasis on the importance of the political radicals, especially the revolutionary wing of the radicals, in the working class. One part of that interpretation involves the machine-breaking (Luddism) in Nottinghamshire, Yorkshire and Lancashire in 1811 and 1812. Thompson does not view this activity as simple industrial protest, as the earlier labor historians did; he argues that it also had political motives. In his remarks on Lancashire Luddism, he attacks the book by the Hammonds,* The Skilled Labourer, *for its narrow, unsympathetic approach, and makes a rather convincing case for Luddism's connections to the constitutional-reform and revolutionary movements.*

What is most noticeable in the Hammonds' handling of the sources is a marked disposition to *commence* their research with the assumption that any bona fide insurrectionary schemes on the part of working men were either highly improbable or, alternatively, wrong, and undeserving of sympathy, and therefore to be attributed to a lunatic, irresponsible fringe. But it is difficult to see why, in 1812, this should be assumed. With a year's intermission, war had continued for almost twenty years. The people had few civil and no trade union liberties. They were not gifted with historical clairvoyance, so that they might be comforted by the knowledge that in twenty years (when many of them would be dead) the middle class would secure the vote. In 1812 the weavers had experienced a disastrous decline in their status and living standards. People were so hungry that they were willing to risk their lives upsetting a barrow of potatoes. In these conditions, it might appear more surprising if men had *not* plotted revolutionary uprisings than if they *had;* and it would seem highly unlikely that such conditions would nourish a crop of gradualist constitutional reformers, acting within a Constitution which did not admit their political existence.

At the least, one might suppose that a democratic culture would approach the predicament of such men with caution and humility. In fact, this has scarcely been the case. Several of the historians who pioneered the study of this period (the Hammonds, the Webbs and Graham Wallas) were men and women of Fabian persuasion, who looked back upon the "early history of the labor movement" in the light of the subsequent Reform Acts, and the growth of TUC and Labour Party. Since Luddites or food rioters do not appear as satisfactory "forerunners" of "the labor movement" they merited neither sympathy nor close attention. And this bias was supplemented, from another direction, by the more conservative bias of the orthodox academic tradition. Hence "history" has dealt fairly with the Tolpuddle Martyrs, and fulsomely with Francis Place;[1] but the hundreds of men and women executed or transported for oath-taking,[2] Jacobin conspiracy, Luddism, the Pentridge and Grange Moor risings,[3] food and enclosure and turnpike riots, the Ely riots and the Laborers' Revolt of 1830,[4] and a score of minor affrays, have been forgotten by all but a few specialists, or, if they are remembered, they are thought to be simpletons or men tainted with criminal folly.

But for those who live through it, history is neither "early" nor "late." "Forerunners" are also the inheritors of another past. Men must be judged in their own context; and in this context we may see such men as George Mellor, Jem Towle, and Jeremiah Brandreth[5] as men of heroic stature.

[1] The Tolpuddle Martyrs were a group of laborers from Tolpuddle who formed a trade union, were discovered, prosecuted and transported from England in 1834. Francis Place was a leading constitutional reformer from the 1790s through the 1830s, and the greatest archivist of the early movement.—Ed.
[2] Oath-taking implies membership in a secret society, usually of a conspiratorial nature. Such societies were numerous in the late 1790s and early 1800s.—Ed.
[3] Small, pitifully armed, attempted risings by the radical workers of Pentridge, Nottingham, in 1817, and of Grange Moor, Yorkshire, in 1820.—Ed.
[4] Agricultural workers' revolts in 1816 and 1830.—Ed.
[5] George Mellor and Jem Towle were workers who led Luddites in Yorkshire in 1812 and 1814, respectively. Jeremiah Brandreth was a worker and a leader of the Pentridge Rising of 1817.—Ed.

Moreover, bias has its way of working into the very minutae of historical research. This is particularly relevant in the matter of Lancashire Luddism. There is only one reason for believing that the various depositions in the Home Office papers as to its revolutionary features are false, and this is the assumption that any such evidence is *bound* to be false. Once this is assumed, the Hammonds embark upon the seas of historical fiction. Thus, the most regular Lancashire informant, in Luddite and postwar years, was an individual designated as "B." This "B" had possibly been employed as an informer since 1801 or 1802,[6] and he was in the confidence of Manchester ultra-Radicals. His name was Bent, and he was a small trader, described in 1812 as "a buyer and seller of cotton waste."[7] As a man of comparative affluence, he was frequently nominated as Treasurer to different secret committees—an admirable listening-post for a spy. On the face of it, he was well-placed to provide inside information.

In *The Skilled Labourer* "B" appears frequently, in the role of a sensationalist and a *provocateur:*

> The Home Office Papers contain numbers of illiterate communications from him, full of lurid hints of the approaching outbursts of the lower orders, encouraged by mysterious beings in high stations. The general rising, with the number of thousands who have taken the oath in different parts of the country, is his constant theme.

The Lancashire Luddite oath (declare the Hammonds), "it is not unreasonable to suppose . . . originated in B.'s fertile brain." When confronted with evidence that a delegate from Manchester visited a secret committee of the Stockport weavers, and sought to involve them in revolutionary preparations, the Hammonds find the convenient explanation:

> Now nobody who has read through the Home Office Papers for this period can fail to recognize in the report of what the Manchester delegate said, the voice of "B.". . . .

Upon this hypothesis (supported by the assumption of superior

[6] See *The Skilled Labourer,* pp. 67, 73. . . . It is not absolutely certain, however, that this was the same "B," since other "B's" were employed—for example, Barlow. . . .
[7] Deposition of H. Yarwood, 22 June 1812, in H.O. 40.1. He was also described as "a respectable cotton-merchant": see *The Trial at Full Length of the 38 Men from Manchester* (Manchester, 1812), p. 137.

knowledge which few readers will care to question) the fiction of provocation is elaborated. But a few pages later, when it suits these same authors to give credence to another part of "B"'s reports, they blandly inform the reader: "That Bent ever seriously tried to induce any of his colleagues to work for violent measures is unlikely, as otherwise men of the stamp of John Knight would not have continued to trust him. . . ." In short "B"'s reports are bent in any way which happens to suit the legend of the moment.[8]

One may suggest that the Home Office papers may be read differently. Bent was not a provocateur, he was a plain informer, and he limited his own activities to what was necessary to secure the continued confidence of his fellow Radicals. He appears to have been a somewhat stupid but observant man, a not unusual combination. Hence his evidence can only be trusted when he describes events in which he participated himself, whereas in his reports of ulterior aims or of organization in the rest of the country he passed on the boasts of some of the more sanguine agitators. The suggestion that Bent was the Manchester delegate who involved the Stockport committee in conspiratorial plans will not stand up to examination.[9]

In fact, if we cease following the false scent of provocation, it is possible to piece together a more coherent account of the inner history of Lancashire Luddism, using very much the same sources as employed by the Hammonds. First, we must recall that Jacobinism had struck deeper roots in Lancashire than in any other manufacturing district, and it had been given a particularly revolutionary tone by the Irish immigration. In Lancashire, almost alone, there is an unbroken thread of *open* antiwar and reform agitation, from the 1790s, through the "United Englishmen,"[10] to the time of Luddism. In 1808 this agitation was reported, not only from Manchester, but from Royton, Bolton and Blackburn. "Is it not time," questioned some Bolton weavers, when announcing their intention to demonstrate every Sunday for two months on Charters Moss above the town,

8 Ibid., pp. 274–5, 297, 336–7.

9 Throughout the early Spring of 1812 "B" reported regularly and garrulously. The Hammonds rest their account of the Stockport meeting, in February, upon the confession of Thomas Whittaker in H.O. 42.121. But "B" reported on 25 March that he still had not succeeded in gaining entry to any of the secret meetings although he hoped to be admitted shortly (H.O. 40.1). He did succeed in attending several of the weavers' meetings in April, but was excluded from an important meeting in May because of a dispute about money (deposition of Yarwood, H.O. 40.1).

10 An underground revolutionary society, connected to the United Irishmen, dating from the late 1890s.—Ed.

> *to drag the British Constitution from its lurking hole, and to expose it in its*
> *original and naked purity, to show each individual* the laws of his fore-
> fathers?[11]

Year by year, the weavers' fruitless agitation for a minimum wage
had driven them in the direction of political agitation, whether of a
revolutionary or constitutionalist character.

In the second place, when Luddism commenced in 1811–12, illegal
trade unionism was already strongly rooted in Lancashire. We have
already noted the degree of organization and consultation of the
artisan trades and of the cotton-spinners in Manchester. The weavers' organization, also, was probably extensive and firmly based. In
towns and even in some villages in Lancashire there were more or
less representative "secret committees" of weavers, accustomed to
consulting with each other on applications to Parliament, petitions,
the raising of funds, etc.[12]

Thus when Luddism came to Lancashire it did not move into any
vacuum. There were already, in Manchester and the larger centers,
artisan unions, secret committees of the weavers, and some old and
new groups of Painite Radicals,[13] with an ebullient Irish fringe. Lancashire was a rich field for spies and *provocateurs,* not because there
was so little, but because there was so much afoot. And the reports
are contradictory, not because all the informers were lying, but because there were contradictions in the movement. In a district which
was, relatively, as politically sophisticated as Lancashire, there were
bound to be divided counsels as to the value of machine-breaking.
This conflict in the workers' councils caused much friction between
February and the end of April 1812. Thus it would seem that at some
time in February the policy of Luddism proper was endorsed by
delegate meetings of the weavers, representing secret committees
in several towns. According to the deposition of one Yarwood, who
was himself a subdelegate of the Stockport secret committee, the

---

[11] See Aspinall, op. cit., pp. xxiii, n. 2; 98–9, n. 1; 100–1, n. 2.
[12] See the evidence of A. B. Richmond. . . . There is also a full deposition in the
Fitzwilliam Papers, F. 46(g) as to a shadowy "weavers' union," said to stretch "from
London to Nottingham, and from thence to Manchester and Carlisle," bound by the
strictest secrecy, with different degrees of oaths at different levels of the organization, extreme precautions in the transmission of papers—the night assignation on
the moor, the message left in a hollow stick in the corner of a designated field, and
so on.
[13] Radicals who believed in the ideals of political democracy expressed by Thomas
Paine, especially in *The Rights of Man* (1791–1792).—Ed.

weavers were enrolled (and "twisted in" with oaths) into an organization whose aims were the destruction of steam looms, the collection of money for arms, and the repulsion of force by force. Subscriptions of 1d a week were collected, and a full-time organizer was actually employed for a month or two, in John Buckley Booth, a former "dissenting minister."[14] But at this point Yarwood's statement becomes vague. It seems that other trades, notably the spinners, tailors and shoemakers, had representatives on the secret committees of Manchester and of Stockport, and that many others than weavers were "twisted in." But the actual plans of the committees were not known to Yarwood, who was secretary only to a district of the Stockport organization, and who delivered his money and received his instructions from John Buckley Booth.

It is clear, however, from Yarwood's account, as well as others, that the committees were divided. As early as April 5 the Manchester committee refused to "Lud":

> Nothing but Discord reigned amongst them that night. Not money sufficient was produced by the Districts to pay what trifle of liquor had been had by the Secret Committee.

It was necessary to raise the money required to send delegates to Bolton and Stockport "to inform them that Manchester would not act in concert" by borrowing it (at Yarwood's suggestion) from "Mr. Bent . . . whom I had seen with the Secret Committee at the Prince Regent's Arms." The riots of mid-April would appear, in most cases, to have been spontaneous affairs, not prompted (or even supported) by the secret committees. By the end of April the Manchester trades (notably the spinners and tailors) refused to pay further money, as a result of which the Manchester delegates (including Bent) were excluded from an important delegate meeting at Failsworth on May 4.

From this time forward, there appear to have been two simultaneous (and perhaps overlapping) forms of organization in Lancashire. On the one hand, one part of the movement concentrated upon renewing the agitation for peace and parliamentary reform. Bent reported a delegate meeting held to prepare a petition for this purpose on May 18, attended by representatives from several towns in both Lancashire and Yorkshire: as usual, he managed to get himself nominated as Treasurer. This was the agitation with which John

---

[14] Perhaps local preacher?

Knight and the "thirty-eight" were associated, who were arrested by Nadin in Manchester in June (as a result of Bent's information) and charged with administering oaths. On the other hand, another part of the movement was certainly engaged in insurrectionary preparations. As early as March 28 Bent claimed to have had a meeting with Irish conspirators, "dangerous daring fellows, and no less than four of them had been in the Rebellion in Ireland." In April he claimed that an Irish delegate had actually visited him, having passed through Dublin, Belfast and Glasgow, and intended to continue his journey to Derby, Birmingham and London. He claimed to have been an officer in the rebellion, called himself Patrick Cannovan, and was "about forty, a genteel appearance, well-drest in black with Hessian boots." Bent's next visitor was a Birmingham delegate, who passed through Manchester on his way to Glasgow via Preston and Carlisle. A further delegate visited one of the committee in mid-May, from Newcastle in the Potteries, bringing the news that several thousands were sworn in and armed in his district, but that London was "very backward . . . it is not carried on with that spirit as could be expected." Those in the conspiracy in London were "chiefly Spitalfields Weavers and Taylors," or "Knights of the Needle."

There is no inherent improbability in these stories of an underground, whose main channel of communication was by way of Irish refugees of 1798. It is mistaken, however, to attempt to divide the picture too sharply into constitutional reformers here and insurrectionary Irish there. It is equally possible that the more sophisticated political reformers regarded themselves as being more serious revolutionaries than the machine-breakers.[15] "The Executive," Bent wrote early in May,

> recommends the people to be peaceable, and not to disturb the peace on any account—those people who do are not of those who are twisted in. . . .

"The fact is," wrote an anonymous Jacobin from Lancaster on May 6, signing himself "Tom Paine,"

> that there is a regular, general, progressive organization of the people going forward. They may be called Hamdenites, Sidneyites, or Paineites. It has fallen to my lot to unite thousands. We—for I speak in the name of multitudes—I say we deny and disavow all, or any connection with

---

[15] Cf. Peel's comment on the reaction of the Halifax democrats to the assassination of Horsfall: "Assassination found no advocate or defender in the old democrat Baines." Peel, op. cit., p. 164.

machine-breakers, burners of factories, extorters of money, plunderers of private property or assassins. We know that every machine for the abridgement of human labor is a blessing to the great family of which we are a part. We mean to begin at the Source of our grievances as it is of no use to petition, we mean to demand *and* command *a redress of our grievances. . . .*

One may suggest that by May 1812 Luddism in both Lancashire and Yorkshire had largely given way to revolutionary organization, which was effecting contact, through the medium of Irish emigrés and old Jacobins, with many centers (Sheffield, Barnsley, Birmingham, the Potteries, Glasgow) where no Luddite outbreaks took place. Of Luddism proper, only the name of the General survived. Rough hand-blocked cards, as well as tallies and secret signs and passwords, were used to secure admission to meetings. An even more tantalizing piece of evidence consists of papers claimed to have been picked up on the road shortly after the Luddite attack on Foster's mill at Horbury, near Wakefield. These consist of two long addresses, in flowery libertarian rhetoric, together with a "Constitution" and "Oath" which are *identical with those discovered upon an associate of Despard,* and cited in evidence at his trial. Unless we suppose some deliberate "plant" (and there is no reason to suppose this), this points unmistakably towards some link between the underground of 1802 and that of 1812.[16]

The evidence as to some kind of underground of this sort comes, in fact, from so many different sources that if it is all to be discounted we must fall back upon some hypothesis which would strain credibility a great deal further—such as the existence of a veritable factory of falsehoods, turning out complementary fantasies, for the sole purpose of deluding the authorities. Thus a quite different informer, a weaver designated "R.W.," told his local J.P. early in June that a Lancashire delegate meeting had been held in Stockport, attended by men from Nottingham, Derby and Huddersfield. These delegates blamed

> *the hastiness of the People here in beginning the Riots before the time appointed, and before they were sufficiently numerous and furnished with arms.*

16 Oliver reported a West Riding delegate meeting (28 April 1817): "I found there were many among them who did not hesitate to say they were well prepared with Despard &c. in 1802, and that Job was lost entirely by the loss of a few who had neglected to keep up a close Communication between them." Oliver's "Narrative," H.O. 40.9.

Pike manufacture was reportedly going ahead in Sheffield, a relatively simple matter in a town with so many small workshops and forges. The rising was now spoken of as planned for the end of September or early October. A midnight meeting was addressed by a "man of genteel appearance" in a field near Didsbury. There was "not a word on mills or machinery," but an appeal for a *general,* instead of a "partial," rising. He was a speaker "as fit to stand up either in the pulpit or at the bar as any man in the kingdom."[17]

But it is at the point where we encounter rumors of *national* organization and "genteel" leaders that we must be most cautious. Obviously, the genuine agitators sought to bolster the morale of their followers with large promises as to national support or even personalities (Cartwright, Burdett, Cochrane, Whitbread, Colonel Wardle and others) who were expected to aid the revolution. But whatever shadowy links the weavers' union, the "Knights of the Needle," or traveling Irish delegates provided, it is certain that Luddism was a movement without national leadership or center, and with scarcely any national objectives beyond common distress and the desire to overturn the Government. Above all, the talk (which such men as Bent passed on) of a "Grand Committee" in London was wholly illusory, and showed a misunderstanding among the provincial revolutionaries as to their true predicament.

General Maitland was probably right when he declared that there was "no real bottom" to Luddism, and that:

> at present the whole of these Revolutionary Movements are limited to the lowest orders of the people generally; to the places where they show themselves; and that no concert exists, nor no plan is laid, further than is manifested in the open acts of violence that are daily committed.[18]

We may accept this judgment, provided that we attend closely to what is being said. Less well informed observers than Maitland frightened themselves because they could not conceive of a "Revolutionary Movement" which did not have some inner knot of "evil, designing

---

[17] This discussion of Lancashire Luddism is largely based on statements of Bent, Yarwood, Whittaker, "R.W." magistrates' reports and anonymous letters in H.O. 40.1 and 42.121 and 42.123.
[18] Darvall, op. cit., p. 175. Cf. Beckett to Maitland, 29 August 1812: "there must be more simultaneous cooperation and more system in what they do before any serious mischief need be feared from them," H.O. 79.2.

men," some aristocratic or middle-class leaders, who were secretly inspiring the whole. When no such conspirators could be found, opinion swung to the opposite extreme: if there were no directors, then there could have been no revolutionary movement at all. It was inconceivable that croppers, stockingers and weavers should attempt to overthrow authority on their own.[19] "There was, it seems, no evidence to prove a *setting on; no* evidence to prove a *plot."* So Cobbett commented on the Report of the Secret Committee of the House of Commons in 1812. "And this is the circumstance that will most puzzle the ministry. They can find no *agitators.* It is a movement of the *people's own."*[20]

It was a movement, however, which could engage for a few months 12,000 troops, and which led the Vice-Lieutenant of the West Riding, in June 1812, to declare that the country was taking the "direct Road to an open Insurrection":

> . . . *except for the very spots which were occupied by Soldiers, the Country was virtually in the possession of the lawless . . . the disaffected outnumbering by many Degrees the peaceable Inhabitants.*[21]

From one aspect, Luddism may be seen as the nearest thing to a "peasant's revolt" of industrial workers; instead of sacking the *chateaux,* the most immediate object which symbolized their oppression—the gig-mill or power-loom mill—was attacked. Coming at the close of twenty years in which the printing-press and the public meeting had been virtually silent, the Luddites knew of no national leadership which they could trust, no national policy with which they could identify their own agitation. Hence it was always strongest in the local community and most coherent when engaged in limited industrial actions.

Even while attacking these symbols of exploitation and of the factory system they became aware of larger objectives; and pockets of "Tom Painers" existed who could direct them towards ulterior

---

[19] See *The Historical Account of the Luddites,* p. 11: "An opinion prevailed that the views of some of the persons engaged in these excesses extended to revolutionary measures, and contemplated the overthrow of the government; but this opinion seems to have been supported by no satisfactory evidence; and it is admitted on all hands, that the leaders of the riots, although possessed of considerable influences were all of the laboring classes."

[20] Cole, *Life of Cobbett,* p. 180.

[21] Darvall, op. cit., p. 310.

aims. But here the tight organization which served to destroy a mill or stocking-frames was no longer of such service; there was no Old Sarum[22] in their community which they could pull down, and the Houses of Parliament were beyond their reach. Undoubtedly the Luddites of different districts reached out to each other; and undoubtedly, in Yorkshire and Nottingham, some kind of district leadership, known only to a few of the "Captains" like Towle and Mellor, was established. But if, as is likely, the accounts of delegate meetings at Ashton, Stockport and Halifax are true, it was here that Luddism was at its weakest—most open to penetration by spies, and most given to frothy talk about insurrections with the aid of the French, Irish or Scots. Only in mid-summer 1812 does it appear that a serious conspiratorial organization was coming into existence, which had detached itself from limited industrial grievances and was extending into new districts. By August (in Captain Raynes' view) the Luddites must either "make a desperate effort to rise in a body," or else the movement must collapse.[23] Two causes brought it to an end. First, the repeal of the Orders in Council, and a rapid improvement in trade. Second, the increasing pressure of the authorities: more troops, more spies, more arrests, and the executions at Chester and Lancaster.

From another aspect we may see the Luddite movement as transitional. We must see through the machine-breaking to the motives of the men who wielded the great hammers. As "a movement of the *people's own,*" one is struck not so much by its backwardness as by its growing maturity. Far from being "primitive" it exhibited, in Nottingham and Yorkshire, discipline, and self-restraint of a high order. One can see Luddism as a manifestation of a working-class culture of greater independence and complexity than any known to the eighteenth century. The twenty years of the illegal tradition before 1811 are years of a richness at which we can only guess; in particular in the trade union movement, new experiments, growing experience and literacy, greater political awareness, are evident on every side. Luddism grew out of this culture—the world of the benefit society,

[22] Old Sarum was the most notorious of the "rotten boroughs"—electoral districts where the franchise was restricted to the owners of property. Old Sarum had no inhabitants—seven deeds to property there were handed out before each election, and taken back after.—Ed.
[23] F. Raynes, op. cit., p. 58.

the secret ceremony and oath, the quasi-legal petition to Parliament, the craftsmen's meeting at the house of call—with seeming inevitability. It was a transitional phase when the waters of self-confident trade unionism, dammed up by the Combination Acts,[24] strove to break through and become a manifest and open presence. It was also a transitional moment between Despard and the "Black Lamp" on one hand, and Peterloo[25] on the other. "I am otherised to say," wrote a (probably unauthorized)[26] "Secretary to General Ludd" from Nottingham to Huddersfield on May 1 1812,

> *that it is the opinion of our general and men that as long as that blackgard drunken whoreing fellow called Prince Regent and his servants have anything to do with government that nothing but distress will befall us there [their] foot-stooles. I am further desired to say that it is expected that you will remember that you are mad [made] of the same stuff as Gorg Guelps Juner and corn and wine are sent for you as well as him.*

In the three counties, the agitation for parliamentary reform commenced at exactly the point where Luddism was defeated. In Halifax, even before the trial of Baines, one of the first Unions for Parliamentary Reform was founded. "I have heard you are a Pettitioning for a Parliamentary Reform," George Mellor wrote to a friend, while awaiting trial in York Castle: "I wish these names to be given as follows . . . ." The names of thirty-nine fellow prisoners were enclosed. ("Remember," he added, "a Soul is of more value than Work or Gold.") And, if we follow the logic through to its conclusion, we may credit the exacerbated comment of a Derbyshire magistrate in 1817:

> *The Luddites are now principally engaged in politics and poaching. They are the principal leaders in the Hampden Clubs which are now formed in almost every village in the angle between Leicester, Derby and Newark.*[27]

24 Acts which made unions illegal, dating from 1799.—Ed.
25 Despard was executed as a leader of a secret conspiratorial society known as the Black Lamp in 1803. Peterloo refers to a mass meeting in support of constitutional reform in 1819 which was attacked by soldiers and local militia, leaving eleven dead and hundreds wounded.—Ed.
26 In addition to letters probably emanating from bona fide Luddite groups, the period was productive of a good deal of free enterprise in letter-writing. Among authors whom I have noted are: "Mr. Pistol," "Lady Ludd," "Peter Plush," General Justice," "Thomas Paine," "A True Man," "Eliza Ludd," "No King," "King Ludd," and "Joe Firebrand," with such addresses as "Robin Hoods Cave" and "Sherwood Forest."
27 Radcliffe MSS., 126/46 and 126/127A; *An Appeal to the Nation* (Halifax, 1812); Lockett to Beckett, 12 January 1817, H.O. 40.3.

Roy A. Church and S. D. Chapman

LUDDISM DISTINCT FROM CONSTITUTIONAL REFORM

Roy A. Church and S. D. Chapman are lecturers in economic history at provincial universities in England: Mr. Church at East Anglia, Mr. Chapman at Nottingham. Both have made detailed studies of single industries and groups of industrialists in their local settings. They have shown an interest in labor in the local setting, as well. In an article on Gravener Henson, a constitutional reformer during the Luddite era in Nottinghamshire, they refute Edward Thompson's argument about a link between the Luddites and the constitutional reformers in Nottingham by referring to Henson's expressed opinions on Luddism and his open political activities. Furthermore, they reject Thompson's view that Luddism was a response to the imposition of a laissez-faire political economy, noting that the change had taken place many years earlier. They have only challenged a small part of Thompson's argument (and there may be some question about the validity of their second criticism), but they have pointed the way to the kind of criticism, and positive work, that needs to be done.

There has always been some doubt about the connection between the constitutional movement for the regulation and protection of the hosiery industry, in which Henson was the moving spirit, and the Luddites. Mr. Thompson favors the view that such a connection existed. He writes: ". . . in Nottingham there is an interesting oscillation between Luddite and constitutional protest, and it is possible that both were directed—at least up to 1814—by the same trade union organization in which perhaps Luddites and constitutionalists (probably led by Gravener Henson) differed in their counsels." Later he concludes that Henson shared the Luddites' "advanced political radicalism," and that "Luddism commenced . . . in Nottingham as a form of direct trade union enforcement." Thompson is drawn to this conclusion by two ideas. The first is his belief that "Luddism gave way to constitutional agitation so suddenly that it is impossible not to believe that the new Committee (of 1812) was not at least partly under former Luddite direction." The second is the alleged association of

From Roy A. Church and S. D. Chapman, "Gravener Henson and the Making of the English Working Class," in *Land, Labour and Population in the Industrial Revolution*, edited by E. L. Jones and G. E. Mingay (London, Edward Arnold Ltd., 1967), pp. 137–145. Reprinted by permission of the publisher. Footnotes omitted.

Henson and other leaders with Luddism, and in support of this contention he quotes Felkin's suggestion that "it is not too much to say that there was no trade combination in the three midland counties during the first forty years of the century with which . . . Henson was not acquainted, both as to their leaders and in due time their operations." Thompson also quotes the Hammonds, Darvall, and Patterson, who recognize that the Luddite gangs won the sympathy of most of the laboring population, while the two latter authors also identify support from "the committees of some, at least, of the ephemeral and semi-secret trade clubs of the time." In the absence of definite proof, Thompson considers the circumstantial evidence sufficient for him to conclude that the Luddites were in the mainstream of working-class movements in Nottingham and that Henson and his committee for parliamentary relief were in some way connected with them. The implication is that Henson's organization worked through constitutional channels by day, and by night engaged in industrial sabotage, a view which clearly warrants careful scrutiny.

It is true that some of Henson's contemporaries believed that he had secret connections with the Luddites. Thus in 1814 the Town Clerk wrote to the Home Office: "I have little doubt that the late breaking of frames were directed by the executive committee of the Union of Mechanics . . . ," the "principal leader" of which was named by another correspondent as Gravener Henson. A county magistrate reported that a hosier whose frames had suffered under the hammers of the Luddites felt convinced that the order for demolishing the frames was issued by Henson. These suspicions appeared to be so well founded that in 1817 Henson was placed under arrest in London while planning an appeal for the condemned machine-wreckers. The London *Courier* recorded that "this man Henson has long been an object of dread to the well-disposed inhabitants of Nottingham and its neighborhood, both on account of the leading influence he was thought to have with the Luddites, and his supposed political principles." In a reply to an inquiry from the Duke of Newcastle, a county magistrate described Henson as one who was "supposed to have been a most active agent of the Luddites, one of the contrivers of mischief without engaging personally in it. . . ." It was this report that led to Henson's imprisonment and interrogation by the Home Secretary. Another London newspaper, the *Observer,* went so far as to identify Henson with the Pentrich insurrection of 1817, while even

Francis Place accepted the popular view that Henson was "King Ludd."

How seriously should we treat these reports? If we are to believe the statement of the two London magistrates who were posted in Nottingham in 1812, neither the town nor county magistrates of Nottingham were in touch with the situation. "Nothing," they reported, "could be weaker or founded on less grounds than their ideas." The mere existence of such a "daring conspiracy" as the Union of Framework Knitters was enough to "impress terror on the minds of the manufacturers," a fear which was doubtless linked with Luddism. It is unlikely that Felkin, subsequently a hosier and lace manufacturer, was unrepresentative of many of his fellow employers when he wrote that while Henson was the pivot of local working-class movements there was no evidence to prove that he was in any way connected with the Luddites. The Tory *Nottingham Journal* recorded that its editor was ignorant of Henson's possible association with Luddism, and the editor of the Radical *Nottingham Review* insisted that "we never before heard it even insinuated that the Luddites had any political objects in view—the direct reverse of this was always understood and believed in this neighborhood."

Henson's attitude to Luddism can be readily appreciated by examining his public and private statements on the subject. It is difficult to believe that he could have succeeded in completely concealing his private opinions, since his papers were twice confiscated—by the Nottingham Corporation in 1814 and by the Home Office in 1817. Those papers reveal only antipathy towards the Luddites. Thus when a Leicester lady confused the constitutional movement with the guerrilla campaigns in 1812, he wrote to her at length that in his view the threat to her family was "a glaring outrage on humanity and social order," while the Bill he was pressing Parliament to adopt was "calculated to restore the distracted peace of the three (hosiery-manufacturing) counties"! Elsewhere, Henson later maintained that he had urged the Luddites to "form clubs and combinations" as an "alternative means of obtaining their ends." He also claimed that his own life had been threatened repeatedly by some of the more desperate Luddites "for counteracting their designs, and for the freedom of language I have used at various times against their practices."

The true basis for the division between constitutionalism and Luddism is seen in the economic division of the hosiery-manufacturing

districts, the social and political significance of which has been over-
looked hitherto. The constitutionalists were based in Nottingham and
(to a lesser extent) in Leicester, where the finer and better-paid
branches of the hosiery manufacture were carried on. The corpora-
tions of both towns, though of differing political complexions, culti-
vated the favor of the burgesses, a large proportion of whom were
framework knitters. Perhaps because of this political strength many
of the gentlemen hosiers who lived in Nottingham were liberal in outlook, a fact which was reflected in the poitical life of the town. Nottingham knitters, moreover, possessed a tradition of constitutional
initiative and negotiation which began in 1778, when the framework
knitters had succeeded in electing their own representative to the
House of Commons. As an analysis of the Nottingham Poll Books
helps to indicate, the permanent divisions in local society, if such existed, were between nonconformity and the Established Church, and
between Tories, Whigs and Radicals. During these years magistrates
had shown a willingness to listen to and sometimes support the case
of the workmen against their employers; and when in 1812 the framework knitters applied to Parliament for a regulation of the trade, they
received the approval of most of the hosiers, who, like Henson and
his knitters, appear to have believed that they were acting in the
interests of the *whole* trade.

The Luddites were based in the country districts, in the industrial
villages of Arnold, Basford, Bulwell, Sutton-in-Ashfield, and Ilkeston,
where the common and lower-paid branches of the manufacture were
carried on. In these villages, moreover, owing partly to the exactions
of the bag hosiers whose powers there were greatest, the knitters
lived under conditions which were markedly inferior to those in the
towns. Exploited by the bag hosiers (the small price-cutting manufacturers) and subservient to the squirearchy, the framework knitters
from the villages were blamed by Henson for the knitters' riots that
occurred in Nottingham in 1779, when according to Henson "the rude
and enraged country people . . . came into the town in large numbers" to precipitate disturbances. The account in the *Nottingham
Journal* of the riots which took place in 1790 suggests that the country workers were once more expressing their discontent, and it was
this volatile section of the population in the hosiery districts, some of
whom considered their interests to be neglected by the knitters of the
town committee, that increased Henson's difficulties in conducting

the affairs of his organization. An illuminating comment was made by a manager of a worsted mill at Arnold in 1808 when he noted that the local people were "more earnest after news than any I know of. They are either mad with joy, or half-dead with disappointment." John Blackner, another prominent member of local working-class movements, himself a migrant from the manufacturing village of Ilkeston in Derbyshire, recorded that the Luddite movement began with a meeting of the country knitters in Nottingham Market Place, and that these people were responsible for machine-wrecking in the area. All of the men convicted of this offense hailed from the villages, as did Jeremiah Brandreth, leader of the Pentrich uprising of 1817. In Nottingham itself few frames were broken. In view of this evidence it seems that a more plausible interpretation of the significance of the oscillation between constitutionalism and violence is that the country knitters took to smashing frames when the established leadership, which was in the hands of Henson and his associates in the town, either failed or was discredited.

Such an interpretation, especially with respect to Henson's role, receives further support from what little we have been able to discover of Henson's political activities. There are few reliable reports of his political utterances, but he is known to have spoken at "respectable" public meetings in 1813 and again in 1817, when the Mayor presided. Henson's presence and the tenor of his speeches on these occasions, when he criticized the Government for continuing the war with France and attacked aristocratic manipulation of membership of the House of Commons, identified him with the Radical leaders of the town. Such a situation is not surprising in view of the town's political history. In the closing years of the eighteenth century Nottingham's ruling oligarchy became fiercely radical and its members made every endeavor to recruit popular support for its democratic reform program. In fact the Corporation succeeded in retaining the political allegiance of a majority of the working classes until the seductive oratory of Feargus O'Connor exploited local hostility against the new Poor Law. Henson's trade-union colleague, John Blackner, editor of the *Nottingham Review* from 1809 to 1816, could command a considerable following among the radicals of the town; an unstinting admirer described him as "more than a match for half the great school-made men in the kingdom," and while Luddism was condemned in the columns of the *Review,* Charles Sutton, its out-

spoken proprietor, showed himself to be sympathetic to radical movements. The important point is that within the locality of Nottingham
and district there was no need for Henson and his circle to resort to
mask-and-hammer politics; within the limits possible when a country
is at war, the views of the working class, like those of other sections
of the community, could find outlets for expression, and through the
correspondence columns of the newspapers their grievances and
aspirations were subjects for public debate.

Furthermore, an examination of the correspondence of Henson's
Committee on industrial matters suggests that we can pursue this line
of argument further. The letters show that the Committee were count-
ing on support from all parts of the hosiery manufacturing districts of
the Midlands. This naive confidence proved to be misplaced, and
indeed in view of the history of labor relations in the area between
1790 and 1811 it is difficult to understand how the Committee made
such an error of judgment. From the 1790s the various branches of the
hosiery industry had taken to negotiating separate wages claims with
the hosiers. In the common, or plain, branch the initiative was invariably taken by country knitters at Basford, Arnold, Ilkeston, or Sutton,
the largest of the country manufacturing villages. Not surprisingly,
these villages were unresponsive to the efforts of the Nottingham
Committee in 1811. A delegate from Basford wrote to the Committee
explaining the feeling in his village that the interests of the plain
branch were being neglected. He complained that the London delegates were "lace and plain silk hands." However, while the village
knitters were uncooperative, considerable support was forthcoming
from hosiers. The conclusion seems inescapable that the division
between the constitutionalists and Luddites reflected the differences
within a trade in which the interests of artisans were sometimes
closer to those of the merchant hosiers than to those of the semi-
skilled workmen in the country districts.

The question remains as to the ultimate aim of the Midland Luddites. Was their purpose, as Thompson maintains, to demonstrate
opposition to "the imposition of the political economy of laissez-faire
upon and against the will and conscience of the working people"?
Or was it, as it has been argued elsewhere, merely the most militant
form of industrial action which minority groups, seeing no alternative
means of redress, resolved to pursue? There can be no doubt that
the Luddites were selective in their destructive forays; they struck

only at wide frames making cut-ups, and at frames which belonged to hosiers and masters who paid framework knitters less than statement price as formerly agreed upon by employers and workmen. In 1814 a letter, signed by "Edwin Lud," which appeared in the *Nottingham Review,* ended: ". . . in the presence of the Almighty God we three times wished Hell might be our external Damnation if we did not . . . if we are not raised eight pence next Friday." According to Henson, the Luddites broke the frames "merely because it was the only means that presented itself, as they conceived, [to escape] from the combinations of their masters." It would seem, therefore, that the actions of the Luddites were calculated only to achieve limited industrial gains.

Thompson admits that, compared with the Luddites of the North, Country Luddism in the Midlands was more confined to industrial objectives. Nevertheless, he stresses that whereas an "otiose 'economist' explanation" which seeks to relate Luddism with bad trading conditions at the end of the wars illuminates the occasion for Luddism, it does not explain its character. For the significant features of Luddism, in Thompson's view, is its occurrence "at the crisis point in the abrogation of paternalist legislation and in the imposition of political economy of laissez-faire upon and against the will and conscience of the working people. . . . Luddism can be seen as a violent eruption of feeling against unrestrained industrial capitalism." This intepretation presupposes that important changes in the manner in which the hosiery trade was conducted must have occurred during the years immediately preceding the Luddite outbreaks. But the work of Professor Chambers has shown that those stockingers who owned their own frames had become a minority even before the final quarter of the eighteenth century, while the apprenticeship system had likewise broken down some eighty years before this time; the inability of the Company of Framework Knitters to enforce its regulations on the hosiers and stockingers of the Midlands was one of the factors which had encouraged the growth of framework knitting in that area during the early years of the eighteenth century. The wage agreements of the 1770s and 1780s were negotiated by workmen's combinations and associations of employers, and lacked the sanction of outside authorities. Certainly the failure of hosiers and knitters, and lace manufacturers and lace makers, to renegotiate wage agreements may warrant a condemnation of hosiers for refusing to meet the framework knitters, and may justify criticism of the lace manufacturers for placing the onus of securing the agreement of all manufacturers upon the shoulders of the workmen's organization. However, this failure does not reflect a recent change from an industrial system based on mutuality and paternalism to one in which competition and laissez-faire dominated economic affairs: such a transformation had long since taken place in the textile trades of the East Midlands.

Peter N. Stearns
EARLY STRIKE ACTIVITY IN FRANCE

Peter N. Stearns was at Rutgers University and is now at Carnegie-Mellon University. He is managing editor of the Journal of Social History. *He has been a remarkably prolific writer, both in terms of the number of books and articles he has written and in terms of the breadth of his interest in the labor and social history of modern Europe. Like Edward Thompson, he approaches labor history from the bottom up; unlike Thompson, he deemphasizes political factors and emphasizes industrial, economic and social factors in economic activism. In the following selection, he explains why most early industrial workers in France did not strike—and why some did. While he is willing to give considerable weight to government repression as a deterrent to activism, he gives virtually no weight to radical ideologies as an encouragement. Rather, he underscores the effect of the structure and prosperity of industry and the economic, social and psychological condition of workers. His analytic method, applied to long periods of strike activity, is a useful one, though it cannot replace detailed studies of local strikes. Indeed, some detailed studies have contradicted Professor Stearns's conclusions about ideology and immigration.*

Any explanation of strike movements by factory labor must . . . cover the two aspects of protest activity. On the one hand, it must account for the infrequency and weakness of agitation by most industrial workers. At the same time, it must show why much greater labor power existed in a very few cases. Fortunately, such an explanation

From Peter N. Stearns, "Patterns of Industrial Strike Activity in France During the July Monarchy," *American Historical Review,* vol. LXX, no. 2 (January 1965), pp. 382–392, by permission of the author. Footnotes omitted.

is possible. It can be shown that, while there were certain general factors inhibiting strike activity in all cases, there were other factors affecting much of the textile industry, and metallurgy and machine building, far more than they affected coal mining and the southern wool industry. The general factors account for the fact that labor even in the exceptional cases was badly organized and relatively lethargic. The special factors explain why a few groups of workers were able to stand out so notably compared to most industrial labor in the July Monarchy itself.

The two most obvious general factors operating against all labor activity were the attitudes and policies of government and industrialists. The national government had long held strikes to be illegal and stiffened the provisions against worker and other associations during the July Monarchy. The cabinet ministers concerned with such matters were unanimous in fearing strikes as hostile both to proper economy and to the stability of the government itself. Some officials were even more inflexible in their stance than most industrialists, and, when the latter occasionally yielded to a strike, the government could be loud in its denunciations of their weakness. To be sure, some prefects occasionally saw the justice of the strikers' demands and attempted to promote at least a compromise settlement. This occurred, for example, in a weavers' strike in Rennes in 1839; the prefect held that wages were unjustly low and induced the employers to yield. More commonly, however, the government reacted to a strike by sending soldiers and arresting and prosecuting the leading workers involved. A large number of strikes, including mining strikes and other vigorous efforts, were only broken up by troops who were perfectly willing to use arms against the strikers. A substantial number of strikers were brought to trial, and while they seldom suffered sentences of more than a year, their example was undoubtedly sufficient to intimidate many prospective strikers. In 1832, for instance, 522 workers were brought to trial, with 304 actually sentenced. Furthermore, several more general governmental policies inhibited strike action. The enforcement of the *livret* as virtually a license to obtain a job, with the possibility open to employers to withhold it in cases of bad conduct, was a powerful means of controlling worker behavior generally, though it was not universally utilized. The common effort by local governments to send away unemployed workers during slumps was another powerful deterrent to coordinated protest during the worst times. In general, government viewed workers with great distrust and acted accordingly to control and to intimidate. Though not all workers were always or equally deterred, most were powerfully influenced by the government's policies.

Even more immediate to most workers was the power exercised over them by their employers. Quite obviously, almost all employers hated and feared strikes. In their eyes, strikes were symptoms of ingratitude that could only end in worsening the workers' lot by disturbing industry. More important, manufacturers feared the effects that strikes would have on the cost and discipline of labor. They also opposed the interruption of production and the potential violence that strikes represented. Employers were, furthermore, able to implement their hostility to labor agitation. They were often instrumental in calling in troops and seeking prosecution of strikers in the courts. Even more commonly, they simply fired strike leaders, at least temporarily. Occasionally, industrialists in a city facing a generalized strike banded together to fight it, though mutual jealousy often prevented any real coordination. Industrialists in Lodève, for example, in 1845 locked out workers from plants that had not been struck. Later in the strike they even sought to bring in machines to replace the striking workers permanently. On other occasions, these and other industrialists sought to break strikes by importing scab labor. Truly, the power of industrialists, backed by government, to resist strikes and to prevent protest through their ability to intimidate, was impressive. Nothing indicates this more clearly than the fact that most strikes, and particularly industrial strikes, failed completely. Workers faced formidable odds in their protest efforts; small wonder that such efforts were so rare.

Employers possessed another type of authority over many workers that undoubtedly had an effect on limiting strikes. Most industrial enterprises were still small. There were some huge firms, particularly in metallurgy and mining, but even in iron production the average company in the 1840s employed only 51 people. Spinning plants, in both wool and cotton, employed an average of 60–70 workers in the same period, while shops for weaving and other branches of textile production seldom assembled more than 30 or 40 workers. There were only 6,000 firms in France with more than 20 employees, and only 3,200 with more than 50. Many industrialists thus could know most of their workers and through daily relations with them could create an impression of a community of interests in the same work. A number of industrialists, particularly in the larger plants, were interested in a wide range of paternalistic efforts to assist their workers. Company housing, health plans, and the like were fairly common. Many workers were profoundly grateful for these and other efforts and felt a genuine devotion to their employer; sincere expressions of grief by workers at the death of many industrialists was a sign of this sort of feeling. To be sure, many workers, even those who never actively protested, did not feel kindly toward their employer. And some of the most paternalistic companies, such as the big mines, had the worst strike records. However, as one factor among many, employer paternalism, often partially adopted to prevent disorder, undoubtedly helped to turn many workers away from agitation. The exceptionally low strike record of the big metallurgical firms, and the textile firms of the Haut-Rhin, may well have been partially caused by the exceptional interest that the industrialists took in their labor force.

Though both government and employers were important in keeping the level of strikes low, they cannot be regarded as the only factors involved. After all, their power bore on artisans as well as factory workers, but the former managed to agitate far more frequently and with greater organization. Their hostility was just as great during most of the Second Empire as during the July Monarchy, but the pace of labor activity was increased notably. Obviously, some more specific factors must be sought.

The condition of industry during the July Monarchy was an important deterrent to strike activity, particularly of a constructive or offensive variety. A successful strike, winning permanent improvements in conditions, could take place only in a period of prosperity. Only then would industrialists be anxious to continue production in order to take advantage of steady or rising business levels. Only then would they be likely to have a sufficient profit margin to afford, albeit grudgingly, some concessions to their workers. During the July Monarchy a large number of industrial areas were not prosperous. Many of the older regions, such as Cholet, were being bitterly pressed by competition from modern factories. Even such centers as Rheims and Louviers, while able to bear up under competition, were too backward in methods to enjoy extensive prosperity. Workers in these regions might strike, and occasionally did out of desperation, but

their protests would be in vain, and usually they would not bother
to try.

In the more modern centers, such as Mulhouse and Lille, levels
of prosperity were of course far higher. But this advantage was modified by the fact that prosperity was not steady. Excessive competition,
leading to overproduction on occasion, caused five years of major
slumps and a number of other lesser declines during the eighteen
years of the July Monarchy. The instability of the economy affected
industrialists and workers alike. Industrialists even in a boom year
were unlikely to relax their hostility to strikes because concessions
might weaken their position when the apparently inevitable slump
occurred. Workers, for their part, were discouraged from developing
any expectations of real improvement in the future, from developing any long-range plans at all, by the knowledge that a crisis would
come to wipe away any advance. Thus the textile industry particularly, in which most industrial workers were engaged, was dominated
by a mixture of decline and instability—an important factor in dis-
couraging more than occasional and halfhearted protest efforts.

The conditions of industry were, however, less important in inhibiting strike activity than were three related aspects of the conditions of
workers themselves. In the first place, a number of potential worker
leaders were being drained off into the ranks of industrialists or foremen. This early industrial period was still sufficiently open, particularly in the production of textiles, to enable an exceptionally active
worker to set up on his own without too much difficulty. The number
who actually did so was relatively small, but if they had not had this
outlet they might well have turned their energies to their own class.
And the number of workers recruited as foremen and top-grade
workers, while obviously a minority of the whole, was quite large,
particularly since the general lack of training and discipline required
an unusually large number of supervisors. The larger textile factories,
for example, used at least one foreman for each room in the plant;
furthermore, workers such as top-grade spinners and miners were
given supervisory functions. Foremen and top workers alike were
encouraged to represent the interests of management and were distinguished from ordinary workers by salaries at least triple the average in the firm. Finally, a number of workers beyond even those who
had risen believed in the possibility of their own rise to at least
lower-middle-class ranks and were correspondingly disinterested in

specifically worker efforts. Hence many worker groups were deprived of their natural leaders and could not organize or act. And many of the strikes that did occur were essentially leaderless and unplanned. To be sure, the upper echelons of the labor force did not necessarily share the interests of management. In many cases, relatively well-paid and experienced workers such as spinners took the lead in agitation. But there is no record of any involvement of foremen in labor protest, except on occasions when they resisted it out of loyalty to their employers. And in general the opportunity of rising in the industrial hierarchy undoubtedly impeded any sense of labor solidarity on the part of many able workers. In fact, some of the scant agitation that occurred was incited and led by teenagers, who were of course abundantly employed in industry at the time. Several coal strikes were instigated by young coal haulers, rather than the miners themselves. Agitation among textile workers, as in Lille in 1837, was often led by apprentice spinners. In other words, the energy of youth was sometimes substituted for the experience and possible wisdom which, in the person of active, intelligent, and mature workers, were frequently drained away into other pursuits.

Even more important than a partial absence of potential leadership was the fact that almost all workers were too poor and too busy to strike often, or for more than a day or two, or even to strike at all. Most laborers in the textile industry worked thirteen hours a day and were in the plant fourteen or fifteen hours. Metallurgical workers seldom worked more than twelve hours, and miners sometimes worked still less, but the labor was physically harder. With such hours, it was unlikely that many workers had the energy to plan a strike; further, so much time spent under the supervision of foremen and employers was another deterrent to the possibility of real organization. This is undoubtedly one of the principal reasons that the majority of industrial strikes were defensive, unplanned reactions to a specific event.

But the material circumstances of most workers made even this type of strike a risky matter. Even aside from the possibility of losing a job as a result of a strike, most workers could ill afford to lose even a day's pay. Their wages were simply not sufficiently above subsistence needs. Though many urban factory workers earned a bit more than was absolutely necessary to live, they were unable to amass enough savings to carry them for more than two or three days without either work or charity. Few workers had any savings. The average laboring family in 1848, in the unlikely event that illness or unemployment did not limit the employment of either man or wife to less than an entire year, earned 765 francs. Three hundred francs of this went for bread, another 100 or 200 for other food; 150 for rent, heat, and a few furnishings; another hundred for clothes. This was life above the subsistence level, but with no frills and no margin of safety. Certainly there was little chance in this situation to strike for positive improvements in conditions because the risk of failure was great, and the result would simply be precious days of income lost. Only to prevent a worsening of income might a short and passionate protest be launched. During crises, desperation at the prospect of a wage reduction or of unemployment could induce some workers to forget their normal caution. Anger had to be vented, despite the risk of loss of pay. But strikes of this sort were almost invariably brief, again because no prolonged protest could be afforded. And most workers did not strike at all even during crises; rather, they clung tenaciously to what jobs and pay they had. In fact, much of the agitation during crises came not in the form of strikes, but of riots. And in the riots unemployed workers commonly took a prominent role for they had little to lose. A riot by men either without jobs or on short time was, for example, the only agitation by labor in Lille during the crisis of 1837. Workers who had jobs generally kept at them in good times and bad, for survival depended on earning without fail.

Obviously, not all industrial employees were in the same material situation as was the average worker. Some earned more and had correspondingly more margin. There is evidence that, other things being equal, such workers were more likely to strike. In certain areas, such as both Mulhouse and Lille, it was pointed out that the best-paid workers generally led what strikes and agitation as did occur. For similar reasons, spinners in cities were more likely to strike than weavers because they earned more. The strikes by miners in the Saint-Étienne region were far better organized and of longer duration than those of Anzin, largely because Saint-Étienne miners earned over half again as much as their counterparts in Anzin. Lille cotton workers conducted a relatively well-organized strike in 1839, a year of high bread prices but also of high employment; there was reason for complaint, but also some margin to allow the risk of complaint. In the far more severe crisis of 1831–1832, when there was no margin at all, Lille workers were quiescent; in 1846–1847, they risked only a brief bread riot. It is indisputable, then, that the low levels of average conditions prevented strikes and that most strikes aside from brief expressions of misery involved workers enjoying conditions above the average.

Material conditions, however, are not the magic key to an explanation of strike activity in the period. It is impossible to correlate agitation with income levels in any consistent way, even leaving aside the misery riot of a crisis year or a particularly poor area. For the fact is that the best-paid group of industrial workers, those in metallurgy and machine building, almost never struck. Their incomes averaged almost twice the level of industrial pay for adult males; they undoubtedly had the means to strike, but they did not choose to do so. Relatively high income was necessary for a vigorous strike, but its possession was no guarantee that the vigor was present. One final general factor must be sought.

Most industrial workers were new to their jobs, to their urban environment, and to each other. In the most modern industrial centers, the very areas in which standards of living for labor were likely to be above average, the vast majority of workers were of first or at most second generation even in 1848. Even in older centers such as Lille much of the factory labor was new not only to the plant but also to the city. Most of the new work force was ignorant; their literacy rates were far lower than those of native urban populations. In Mulhouse in the 1840s almost three-quarters of the illiterates had been born outside the city. In Lille in 1848 only a tenth of the workers were literate, though many more had had a brief educational experience. Many of the new workers were also unusually impoverished and unhealthy when they entered the factory labor force. Thus they were cut off from much possibility of intelligent protest not only by their lack of education but also often by physical weakness. But most of all they were confused. Their traditions were those of the countryside, which no longer had much meaning for them. In some cases they may have retained peasant habits of resignation. This was fortified, for those who attended church, by constant recommendations of patience and orderliness. It was further fortified by the fact that conditions of factory labor, in terms of income, hours, and the like, represented little deterioration and often positive improvement when compared to conditions in the countryside.

What was most upsetting to the new workers was the change in their psychological environment. The older norms of marriage and family, of religion, and of recreation had less meaning in the factory city. The new and rapid pace of work, the discipline of the factory, the strangeness of the people, and the fact that the members of a family now usually worked apart were far more disturbing than bad food or inadequate clothes. But it was terribly hard to express complaints about such matters. There was no tradition to fall back on, and the people from the country had relied on tradition. There was little motivation to join forces with strangers, who happened to be fellow workers, since the presence of such strangers was one of the newest aspects of factory life. The habit of a substantial minority of workers to return to the country occasionally, especially at harvest-time or during crises, further impeded adjustment to urban conditions and joint action to protest the difficulties of the new life. And there was little chance even fully to realize what the trouble was, since the novelty of the situation was so great. Hence the considerable discontent that undoubtedly existed in the period was expressed primarily in individual ways; the heavy consumption of alcohol, the decline of religious practice, and the increase in crimes against property, including thefts in the plant, were the most important forms of protest. Of necessity, they were individual forms, thus precluding much effort at cooperative action. Many strikes were born or ended in a bar; far more were drowned there. The individual disorientation of a substantial number of the early industrial workers was the final factor inhibiting vigorous strike activity. These workers often felt themselves debased. They lacked the moral energy to rise in protest. Fundamentally apathetic, they relieved any resentment they clearly felt by an occasional bout at the tavern. Beyond this, workers could not think: "When we grow old, the hospital will receive us, or we'll die, and then everything will be over."

A large number of workers had simply lost their accustomed standards and had not found anything to replace them. At most, they attempted to apply some of the canons of rural life to their new situation. This is why so much worker agitation in the newest industrial centers is indistinguishable from peasant riots. In Mulhouse in 1847, in Lille in 1830 and 1847, and in many other regions, the appalling conditions of the industrial slump were protested not by a strike, but by an attack on the bakers. As in peasant agitation, the most immediate apparent villain was attacked, often violently, as the only response to unexpected misery. In fact, the same type of bread riots occurred in a number of rural areas during 1847. The many industrial areas that had little or no worker agitation beyond an attack on food merchants during a famine year were simply areas in which the worker continued at best to apply peasantlike responses to cases of outright hunger. When so clear a grievance was not presented, the worker had no standards to follow. Further, his environment was so different from the rural that even many periods of real misery passed without response.

In addition, then, to the pressure of government and employers, subsistence conditions and the newness of the situation inhibited active labor protest. In the case of most textile centers, these factors were supplemented by the fact that a large minority of the working force was composed of women and children. Both were, naturally, more docile than male workers—one of the reasons for their wide use. Only a few regions escaped the multiple burdens of poverty and disorientation. Metallurgical workers, of course, were not poor; nor were they hampered by many women and children in their ranks. Their industry was far more consistently prosperous than the textile industry, though it had its crises, particularly prior to the building of railroads. Most important, however, was the fact that metallurgical workers were new to their situation for the most part. The most experienced workers were often foreigners, usually British, and were highly paid. They had little contact with most of the new labor. Even so, one of the few metallurgical strikes on record was led by experienced British workers. Aside from the British, skilled workers were either brought in from a number of different parts of France or were newly trained locals. Neither group had sufficient roots in the new situation to feel particularly clear about its needs and strengths. And the unskilled labor that composed over half the work force in new centers like Le Creusot was brought in from the local peasantry. These workers, far more highly paid than ever before in their experience, lacked any real sense of being workers and any grievances that could be expressed in collective protest. In metallurgy there was neither the need for hunger riots or defensive strikes, given the relatively good conditions, nor the experience and orientation necessary for constructive strikes.

There remained coal mining and some of the major southern textile centers, notably Lodève and Castres. Not all the southern centers were involved in intensive strike activity. Carcassonne workers were too poor to strike. Workers in Mazemet, though very near Castres, were located in a new industrial center; they lacked the experience and sense of tradition of Castres and Lodève. Both the latter cities were relatively old wool centers. They brought in some new labor from the outside, but the majority of their labor force was local. This majority represented a nucleus of firm tradition of a semiartisanal nature. Hence the workers of Lodève expressed their desire to return to a purely artisanal organization; they had a memory of past standards and a tradition of craft closeness that would serve them even in a partially mechanized period. In this they differed from their colleagues in northern textile centers. At the same time, their own pay was relatively high, allowing some margin for protest activity. And their employers were engaged in an industry for which there was remarkably steady demand, though crises were not unknown. For both Lodève and Castres produced extensively for the French Army, and government orders could not be ignored, at pain of violation of contract and the loss of vital business. As the workers well knew, therefore, employers would often have to yield to strikes in order to meet definite business commitments. Finally, Lodève and Castres employed fewer women and children than was the average in textile manufacture; their hours of work were also lower by two or more, allowing more time for thought or planning. A group of relatively prosperous male workers, most of them accustomed to their work, their city, and each other, engaged in an industry that was fairly steadily prosperous; such was the formula that induced the exceptional strike activity of Lodève, Castres, and to an extent Bédarieux.

The mining industry presented many similar features. It was far more consistently prosperous than textiles or even metallurgy; hence coal prices fell very little during the July Monarchy. Mineowners were often pressed with orders that they could scarcely fill; in fact, France had to import coal because its domestic production was insufficient. Several miners' strikes took place in periods when manufacturers were swamped with orders. Miners were, moreover, seldom called upon to work more than ten hours and sometimes worked only eight. Their work was, of course, far more tiring than labor in textiles or even metallurgy. But at least their waking hours were not totally devoted to work and travel to work; many miners, for example, were regularly able to spend some time gardening. Correspondingly, they had at least some time away from the job, which could be used for reflection on conditions and for actual organization. Few women and children worked in the mines. Miners earned a wage well above that of textile workers, and usually above subsistence as well. Often they could purchase some garden land; this could be a source of support in time of strike. Miners were not totally new to their work or their area. In the Saint-Étienne region particularly, while some new miners were hired during the July Monarchy, probably only a fifth of the workers in the 1840s were of first generation. At Anzin the labor force was increased by one-third during the July Monarchy, but the company dated from the eighteenth century, and at least half of the labor force consisted of families that had been associated with the company for two generations or more. So with coal mining, too, there was often a large nucleus of workers with a real sense of tradition, in a profession that had long relied heavily on such tradition. Through this tradition the extensive disorientation and confusion that weakened industrial labor generally could be avoided. Interestingly, newer mining regions such as Alais saw no strike activity comparable to that of the more traditional centers. In such regions the skilled workers were imported, and so were new to the area, whereas most of the labor force, recruited locally, was new to the trade; little real sense of tradition could exist. Finally, the mining companies most often struck were huge concerns, remote from the worker. They were less paternalistic and more often exploitative than metallurgical firms of great size. And they were often under public attack because of their size; miners both at Anzin and at Saint-Étienne operated in an atmosphere of widespread public sympathy. These specific factors were simply a further addition to situations already comparatively favorable to strike activity.

Relative prosperity, both of industry and workers, and a sense of tradition were sufficient to allow the few real industrial challenges to government and employers that occurred in the July Monarchy. The same factors were, of course, present in the comparatively active ranks of artisans in Paris and Lyons. They were, further, factors that were likely to become increasingly introduced in the ranks of textile and metallurgical workers as time went on. Both industries, in the more modern centers, tended to become increasingly prosperous and, in many instances, to offer rising standards of living to the workers. Both tended to decrease hours of work in the 1840s, and the textile industry curtailed its use of children in the same decade. Most important, workers in these industries increasingly developed a set of values appropriate to their new situation; they were no longer lost newcomers. Their orientation was often aided by contact with the more traditional and active worker groups. Most of the fruits of these developments were seen only after the July Monarchy had ended; they required more time than the period itself offered. Some halting advance may be seen, however, in a few areas by the 1840s. In Lille, for example, the slump around 1830 had seen only scattered agitation, led, interestingly, by the thread twisters; here a traditional, artisanal group, albeit very ill-paid, was more active than factory labor. By 1839 factory workers were capable of mounting a really organized strike, and they were far more active in the crises of 1847 than they had been in 1830, though their vigor was certainly limited. Similarly, Mulhouse workers reacted more massively to the crisis of 1847 than to that of 1828–1830; admittedly, this may have been partly because the crisis was more severe. The most interesting case of clearly increased activity among textile workers occurred, however, in Elbeuf. This was a relatively prosperous wool center, with a new factory labor force. There was no history of agitation among the workers prior to 1846. In that year and the next, however, guided partly by agitators from Paris, the workers were in considerable ferment. They were led by the spinners, a relatively well-paid group with a long record of docility. Their action consisted of a number of strikes and riots, for the purpose of higher pay and protection against undue mechanization. Under the immediate impulse of the economic collapse, but fortified also by a generation or more of experience in industry, the workers of Elbeuf for the first time frightened both government and employers. Clearly, there is no pervasive trend of heightened worker activity in the July Monarchy itself. But there are indications that some of the causes of labor weakness were being modified, in a few areas at least.

For the July Monarchy as a whole, the impotence of industrial labor remains the outstanding fact. The few factors favoring protest action generally were greatly outweighed by the vast number of inhibiting forces. Some of these forces came from outside labor itself, some from conditions within. In a few cases the confusion and poverty of workers were absent to a sufficient extent to permit unusually active and elaborate labor movements. But even the miners of Rive-de-Gier, even the workers of Lodève, were too poor to afford more than occasional and loosely organized efforts. Even they lacked a clear picture of what they wanted for the future; the workers of Lodève, who could present demands relating to the very structure of their industry, looked really to the past. And against miners and southern wool workers, the force of employers and especially of government troops could always be applied. This outside force could defeat most efforts whenever internal weakness was not sufficient. The miners of Anzin, however, managed to win a number of wage raises through strike action; those of Rive-de-Gier were partially successful. Workers of Lodève and Castres also achieved some gains through strikes. Clearly, the example would spread. For many of the most important weaknesses of industrial labor were not permanent. Time and experience would decrease the debilitating sense of newness. Industry itself would create greater prosperity and so a greater possibility of taking vigorous action. As these factors changed, the external barriers to worker protest would have to yield.

E. J. Hobsbawm
GENERAL LABOR UNIONS IN BRITAIN

Eric Hobsbawm, a Reader in History at the University of London, has opened up whole new areas of working-class and popular history and overturned many orthodox intepretations in the older areas of labor and economic history. Although he has written a number of fascinating books (Bandits, Primitive Rebels), some of his most interesting work appeared in the form of incisive articles. Fortunately he has published a collection of the most important articles. The collection's title reveals the author's intention to look behind labor institutions to find the Labouring Men. *In the following excerpt, he looks behind the general labor unions in Britain from the 1880s to World War I, to see who exactly belonged in different periods. By so doing, he challenges the "myth" of the new unionism as associations of mobile, unskilled laborers, founded by Socialists—a myth propounded by the Socialist union leaders and perpetuated by early Socialist historians. He also provides a history of the development of contemporary general unions in Britain.*

"General labor unions" which enroll all classes of labor, irrespective of skill or occupation, have existed, at some time or other, in most industrial countries. In Britain, where they play a greater part in modern trade unionism than elsewhere, they have been permanently established in strength since the late 1880s. While "general unions" have used many of the bargaining techniques of "craft" unionism in the past, and have increasingly tended to adopt those of "industrial unionism,"[1] they cannot wholly be analyzed in terms of either of these classical divisions of trade union organization. They have, in fact, fulfilled three quite distinct functions—often simultaneously. As *class* unions they have attempted to unite all workers against all employers, generally under socialist or revolutionary inspiration. As *laborers'* unions, they have attempted to provide effective organization for workers incapable of, or excluded from, orthodox craft unionism. As *residual* unions, lastly, they have organized any body of workers not

From E. J. Hobsbawm, "General Labour Unions in Britain, 1880–1914," in his *Labouring Men* (New York, 1963), pp. 211–229. Reprinted by permission of George Weidenfeld and Nicolson Ltd. Footnotes omitted.

[1] By craft union, Hobsbawm means organizations for individual sections of workers, bargaining independently of one another. By industrial unions he means organizations which unite or coordinate the bargaining of all groups whose bargains affect each other.—Ed.

effectively covered by other unions (and some that were). Neither the first nor the third functions call for any special form of organization. Indeed, the modern "class" union—the Industrial Workers of the World in the USA and elsewhere, the One Big Union in Canada, the various communist unions between the wars—have been among the chief propagandists of rigorous "industrial" unionism. But the problem of organizing the "unskilled" and "laborers," where the "skilled" and "artisans" were already in strong and exclusive unions of their own, did demand tactics and policies peculiar to "general" unions. It is with these, and with their changes, that this article will be mainly concerned, though an inquiry into them will also involve some analysis of the actual composition of these unions. The subject is, on the whole, a neglected one.

The unions formed in the expansion of the late 1880s recruited workers of all grades of skill, and adopted numerous forms of organization. Yet it is no accident that the "New Unionism" is normally associated with the great "general" societies, the largest and most prominent bodies produced by the movement—Dockers, Gas-workers, Tyneside Labour Union and a number of others. Most of these have since merged to form the two giant unions of Transport and General Workers and General and Municipal Workers which today include something like a quarter of the total British trade union membership. Yet their history has been by no means one of unbroken success. The absence of reliable statistics makes it impossible to measure the relative and absolute strength of "general" unions in the "New Unionism" of 1889–1892; but their proportionate strength was undoubtedly very great. Like most other "new" unions, they collapsed badly in the depression of the early 1890s; but unlike some others, the "general" societies did not fully recover until after the renewed expansion of 1911–1914. Between the two expansions they appeared to have shot their bolt, and very definitely lost ground. Table I gives a brief comparative picture of the fortunes of various types of "new" unions (all composed of conventionally "unskilled" men) between 1892 and 1912.

It is clear that we have here three patterns: the "craft" societies with their stable (and restricted) membership; the General Unions, fluctuating, but without any marked upward tendency, yet climbing almost vertically after 1911; and the "industrial" or compound unions, growing steadily from 1900, though rather faster after 1911. In, say, 1910 it might have seemed that the second group was destined, if

TABLE I
Membership of Certain Unions 1892–1912 (in thousands);
Average Annual Members over 3- and 2-Year Periods

	1892– 94	1895– 97	1898– 1900	1901– 3	1904– 6	1907– 9	1911– 12
All Unions	1,555	1,614	1,895	2,010	2,058	2,492	3,277
"General"[a]	76	69	88	81	67	74	186
"All-grade"[b]	19	22	29	34	45	60	109
"Local crafts"[c]	12	12	12	12	11	12	24

[a] London Dockers, London Gas-workers, Birmingham Gas-workers, NAUL, National Amalgamated Labourers Union.
[b] London Carmen, Amalgamated Carters, Amalgamated Tram and Vehicle Workers, Municipal Employees, Liverpool Dockers.
[c] London Stevedores, Thames Watermen, Cardiff Trimmers, Mersey Quay and Rail Carters, Winsford Saltmakers.

not to replace, then increasingly to overshadow the third. But in fact, the opposite has happened. Both groups (*a*) and (*b*) have merged to form the two vast general unions of today. We can thus distinguish three phases in the development of the general unions: the expansion of 1889–1892, the relative decline in their importance between 1892 and 1910, and their renewed, and as it turned out, permanent, expansion after 1911. Each of these phases developed its peculiar forms of organization and policy.

The theory in the mind of the founders of the general unions of 1889 (and of their predecessors) was fairly simple. The "laborer," mobile, helpless, shifting from one trade to another, was incapable of using the orthodox tactics of craft unionism. Possessing "merely the general value of labor" he could not, like the "skilled man," buttress a certain scarcity value by various restrictive methods, thus "keeping up his price." His only chance therefore was to recruit into one gigantic union all those who could possibly blackleg on him—in the last analysis every "unskilled" man, woman or juvenile in the country; and thus to create a vast closed shop.

"If we should confine ourselves," said Will Thorne, "to one particular industry, such as gasworks, alone, and if those other people in various parts of the country are let go unorganized, then, if we had a dispute with any of the gas companies, these men would be brought up to be put in our places." Theoretically, therefore, there was no limit to the union and its leaders recognized it. The Tyneside Labour

Union soon became the National Amalgamated Union of Labour. A purely regional body in South Wales called itself the National Amalgamated Union of Labourers of Great Britain and Ireland; the Lancashire Labour Amalgamation became the British Labour Amalgamation, even as its effective radius contracted to some twenty miles from Piccadilly, Manchester. This was not grandiloquence, but—so it was thought—the bare recognition of facts.

Similarly, the acknowledged weakness of "laborers" led them to rely much more than the "artisans" on political pressure and legislative action. Thus a natural alliance sprang up between politically quite immature men seeking to organize certain "weak" groups of workers—dockers, gasworkers, woollen workers, etc.—and the revolutionary socialists of the 1880s, who supplied, or converted, the leaders of most, but not of all, general unions. It would be artificial to draw an exact frontier between those which began as ordinary "trade unions" (like Tillett's Tea Operatives—the ancestor of the Dockers' Union), coming under socialist leadership later, and those formed, like the Owenite unions (and perhaps the National Labour Federation on Tyneside, 1886–1893), as much with trade union ideas as with some wider social or moral transformation in mind. Both unions of "weak" workers, and politico-industrial bodies tended to grow at much the same times of social tension and unrest; and by the late 1880s a body of socialist organizers and propagandists was once again available in Britain. One may, however, guess that the large national and regional "general" unions of 1889 were the offspring of a marriage between the class unionism of the socialists and the more modest plans of the unskilled themselves. The expansion of the early 1870s, in other respects an important—and neglected—forerunner of the "New Unionism," produced unions of a far more sectional type.

This, then, was the theory. One cannot fully understand its weaknesses without reminding oneself of contemporary beliefs about the structure of the working class, above all about that sharp frontier which divided the "skilled" from the "unskilled," the "artisan" from the "laborer." At first sight the sharpness of this division is surprising, for both middle-class and artisan economists believed the rewards of labor (with or without assistance) to be broadly proportional to merit, and to physical, intellectual and moral superiority. A gradually ascending scale, such as that suggested by our division into "unskilled," "semi-skilled" and "skilled" might have appeared more suitable for such views. But, in fact, labor was divided into two groups: the one "differentiated by training and experience, to such an extent that its transference to other occupations would involve, *ceteris paribus,* an appreciable industrial loss," the other "the general mass of rude or unskilled labor," undifferentiated, and not tied to any special occupation.

In the minds of many, this distinction camouflaged a much more old-fashioned one—the preindustrial line between the skilled all-around "craftsman," the genuine maker of things, and the "laborer" who merely fetched and carried for him. Nor was this distinction purely traditional. We have increasingly come to remember how much of the nineteenth-century British industrial organization, at any rate before the age of mass-production and "dilution," was really cast in a preindustrial mold. Builders and engineers, boiler-makers and tailors might still reasonably imagine that they were capable of making houses, machines, ships and clothes without the convenient, but not indispensable, help of the laborer; as a hotel chef could, at a pinch, produce a dinner without the help of the potato-peeler and bottle-washer. Alternatively, their position as sub-contractors or co-employers of the laborers would also lead them to regard the difference between "artisan" and "laborer" as one of kind, not merely, like that between craftsman, improver and apprentice, as one of degree. The higher wages, the greater respect, the other ponderable and imponderable perquisites of the "aristocrat of labor" would thus be interpreted as a tribute to his peculiar excellence; and those groups of semi-skilled who, for one reason or another, succeeded in obtaining them—cotton-spinners, locomotive drivers, some coal-hewers—would readily assimilate their position to that of the "craftsman."

But such groups formed a minority of the organized trades, and before the introduction of the block-vote in the Trade Union Congress of the 1890s, their full numerical weight was in any case not appreciated.

The "artisan-laborer" pattern was thus conventional as much as real; and every industrial and technical change tended, on the whole, to increase its unreality. The "artisans" were all members of groups which exercised effective bargaining strength (though not necessarily because they were skilled or craft-trained). But the "laborers," defined by exclusion, did not necessarily contain only men without such strength; though it was easy to conclude that this was so. On the contrary. The Great Depression saw labor on the defensive, and the leaders of the movement more inclined to reinforce restrictive barriers against blacklegs than to spread trade unionism. Hence, in spite of certain advances of semi-skilled groups towards "artisan" status, by the late 1880s the ranks of the "laborers" contained an increasing number of men immediately capable of orthodox unionism, and often of great bargaining strength. All they required was the impetus to organize, and this the explosion of 1889 gave them. But even the ideal "general laborer" of the Victorian convention— fluid, shifting from trade to trade, doing his undifferentiated fetching and carrying as well or as badly wherever he was put—was probably rather less common than was supposed. Moreover, as mechanization and modern factory methods spread, employers came to doubt whether even he lacked all "special value." The general unions thus found themselves recruiting a great many men who, for one reason or another, commanded that power to make themselves scarce; to cause appreciable loss upon transference, or to be worth inducements for greater efficiency, which were the basis of orthodox bargaining strength; an unexpectedly well-armed force.

This was fortunate for them, for the genuinely floating, or mobile worker, however skilled, was devilishly hard to organize under laissez-faire conditions. Unions composed of such men—the Navvies in Britain, the IWW in America—were content if they could keep a few hundred regular members, and a few regular offices or centers, whence they could recruit a temporary mass membership and exercise temporary job control as and where the fight flared up. The vast national, regional or even local closed shops in which the old General Union saw its salvation were difficult to maintain generally, beyond the first flush of expansion. It is thus not surprising that the leaders of the general unions should have modified their policy. What appears surprising is that they should have been unaware of its inadequacies from the start, and have clung to it for so long.

The official foundation of the unions was the "local branch" comprising all kinds of workers. A more realistic division was based on trades, places of employment and the like. The Gas-workers, pioneer and largest of general unions, provide examples of both. Organization in the fluctuating London area was general, forty-four out of the sixty-one branches in 1897, thirty-seven out of fifty-five in 1906 being so described, or unspecified. It seems clear that these branches grew out of the original nuclei of stokers organized around their local gasworks; but the leader of the union strongly resisted attempts to break up these agglomerations, sometimes thousands strong, into trade branches on the provincial pattern. This had the advantage of allowing them to change character rather than to dissolve if, as gradually happened, the original stokers faded away. Nevertheless, it must have been extremely clumsy, for we constantly find it supplemented by "place of employment" organization of one kind or another. Alone of district secretaries, the London man spent much of his time going around building jobs, coal wharves and factories, checking cards and the like. Some of the clumsiness is indicated by the fact that members claiming compensation against one large contracting firm came from no less than seven branches as far apart as West Ham and Battersea. Shop-stewards, such as the northern Amalgamated Union of Labour allowed its branches, existed, but attempts which were made from time to time—by northern delegates and London builders—to give them official functions other than the simple collection of contributions, were resisted.

Outside London, however, the number of occupational or employment branches outnumbered—outside ports and small towns greatly outnumbered—the general ones, as Table II shows.

It is clear that, from the start, the membership of general unions did not fit easily into an organization designed for the mobile and fluid, and those not tied to individual industries.

How far indeed were the union organizations for the "general" laborer? Since the term is vague, and its meaning varies with region and industry, we cannot say. Moreover, most of our figures refer to branches, and a "general" branch may have consisted not of general laborers, but merely of an assortment of miscellaneous trades, each too small for a separate branch. Broadly, it is clear that the proportion of general laborers went up in time of expansion, or during great strikes, when they flocked into unions. In normal times it might be small. The best figures available, from an occupational list of the NAUL[2] in 1895, give 1,088 out of 11,000 members as "general labor"; two years earlier a similar proportion had belonged to

[2] National Amalgamated Union of Labour (see Table III).—Ed.

TABLE II
Gas-Workers' Union. Number of "General" Branches in Districts
at Various Periods, 1890–1911

District	Year	Total number of branches	"General" Wholly	"General" Partly or unspecified
Birmingham	1896[a]	25	0	0
	1899[a]	33	0	0
	1909	30	1	1
Bristol	1891[b]	10	0	0
	1893	11	0	0
	1896	11	1	0
	1904	8	0	0
Lancs.	1903	41	10	10[b]
Leeds	1890–91	28	2	0
	1891–92	23	9[c]	0
	1896	30	7[c]	0
Mersey	1891	21	9	2
	1896	14	4	0
East coast	1909	33	8–9	0
North-east	1896	16	1	0
	1899	36	4	0
	1904	37	1–2	0

[a] "Birmingham Metal Trade Alliances" in force.
[b] "General" here includes a number of municipal branches; also perhaps some engineering labor. Lancs. described itself as "occupationally organized" until 1911 (NUGMW [1929] Souvenir, p. 26).
[c] Misleading. E.g., in 1896 "general" includes up to six municipal branches and one of steelworks laborers.

general branches in the same union: 2,700 out of 22,000 in thirteen branches out of 103 on the northeast coast, three out of thirteen in Sheffield. One cannot really conclude much from such occasional figures.

One thing, however, is clear. The General Unions, at any rate between 1892 and 1911, depended far more on their foothold in certain industries and large works than on their ability to recruit indiscriminately, hence (one may suppose) on the whole on a stabler and more regular type of worker than they had originally envisaged. Local recognition by employers, of course, reinforced this tendency. Thus in the Leeds district of the Gas-workers the two "recognized" groups of Dyers and Gas-workers made up twelve out of twenty-eight branches in 1891, ten out of twenty-three in 1891–92, sixteen out of thirty in 1896. On the northeast coast the strength of the NAUL in the shipyards—where it was recognized—is well brought out in Table III. Thus while something like half the 1893 strength of branches in general labor dissolved, fifteen-sixteenths of the shipyard strength remained stable. While we have no comparable figures for other unions, it is clear that things were much the same there. The Labour Protection League relied largely on its foothold in Woolwich Arsenal (in addition to its control over specialized grain and timber porters on the docks), the Birmingham gas-workers on their ties with the Corporation, even the small Machine and General Labourers of Bolton noted that "we have gained a substantial foothold with a few employers."

And these were, of course, mainly the large ones. Thus we know that, at a time when the entire 300-odd branches of the Gas-workers had only some 29,000 members, five branches alone of engineering, rubber, bridge-yard, cotton and iron-workers, each of men in a single firm, made up some 3,000 of the total; and district reports make it clear how the entire union could be "carried," especially during a depression, by a few large works branches. It is doubtful whether we can estimate the extent to which general union branches were composed of employees of large works, or of single works. However, the following attempt may just give an order of magnitude, though the after-effects of the slump of 1902–1904 may exaggerate the im-

TABLE III
National Amalgamated Union of Labour. Branches Closed 1896–1900, through Loss of Members

Occupation	Total closed, 1896–1900	Total of branches in occupation, 1893	
		Wholly	Partly
Shipyard workers	3	43	5
Iron and steel	2	8	3
River, waterside	5	13	2
Chemical, lead, copper	4	14	0
Engineering labor	5	10	6
Navvies, builders	3	8	1
General	10	17	4
Others	4	18	4

portance of the large works somewhat. Assuming an equal degree of "concentration" in Barnsley (for which we have no details) as in Nottingham, we find that about half of the union branches outside London were in "large firms." Membership, of course, is likely to have been far more concentrated. The estimate below, in Table IV, is probably on the conservative side.

Having established such footholds, possibly—though we cannot measure the extent—in what J. R. Clynes called "classes of work in which the evil effects of competition could not be felt," the union could ride out bad times. It is quite remarkable, and wholly unlike American unionism, that the general unions were evidently quite as capable of hanging on in industries subject to the trade cycle as elsewhere. True, among the Gas-workers, Bristol, Leeds and Lancashire districts had strong cores of gas and municipal labor; but Birmingham was built around the metal trades, South Wales on tinplate and tubes, the northeast (like the bigger NAUL) on ships and engineering, Barnsley and Nottingham on iron, steel and pit-top men, Hull on docks and shipyards. The Dockers' Union rested largely on tinplate. The point illustrates the importance of "recognition" by the employers. Once a firm tolerated or accepted the union, as the shipbuilders did the NAUL, a slump would not bring the otherwise inevi-

TABLE IV
Gas-Workers' Union, Second Quarter, 1905.
Branches in "Large Firms"*

District	Number of branches	Dec. 1905 Members	Branches with members mainly in "large firms"
Barnsley	22	2,018	?
Birmingham	33	2,346	6–8
Bristol, south-west	20	1,472	5–6
East coast	15	1,644	6
Lancs.	37	4,665	15–20
Leeds	34	4,012	24
London	—	5,758	—
North-east	35	3,801	26–28
Nottingham	10	Incl. in London	7
South Wales	28	2,234	13–14
Total (without London)	234		102–13

* The London area comprises all branches not in separate districts, and the Nottingham branches.

table expulsion and destruction. Clearly, the class-conscious militancy of the early leaders was less likely to commend itself in such a state of affairs than a more cautious and conciliatory policy.

Insensibly, then, policy was modified. The classical "laborers'" union knew perfectly well that it could win little without a strike; at any rate an occasional one. But the NAUL, well dug in on Tyneside, boasted about its freedom from strikes just like the boilermakers. The Marxist Londoners in the Gas-workers' Union continued to demand the abolition of piecework, instead of which they wanted a high-standard living wage; but the men from Birmingham, Lancashire and Llanelly objected. Piecework was becoming increasingly popular, and in any case the tinplate trade had just decided to "follow the machines," i.e., to abandon restriction of output. In the same way, the Workers' Union, whose main strength lay in semi-skilled engineering, was later to support the mechanization against which so many older unions fought.

But there was a more striking change. Like most general unions the Gas-workers had originally dreamed of the eventual unification of all laborers' societies into One Big Union: or, as a second-best, of the universal interchangeability of union cards: "one man, one ticket." From the point of view of shifting or nomadic laborers, moving from job to job and trade to trade, nothing could be more logical. Wherever they went, whatever their union, any ad hoc collection of organized laborers could act as a single society for the purpose of exercising temporary job control. On building sites, for instance, this frequently happened. But since the floating laborer was not really the core of the general union, "one man, one ticket" found an increasingly lukewarm reception from the champions of the alternative tactic, which we may call "one ticket, one job": the local job monopoly. Each union, having perhaps just scraped local recognition, came to regard immigrants, not as reinforcements which enabled it to hold strongpoints in an ever-shifting labor market, but as potential blacklegs. "Take any dock in the country," argued Ernest Bevin in 1914. "What is the serious problem we have to face? It is that where the men have been organized longest, and have been able to build up certain conditions, the employer is always doing his best to attract a big surplus of labor around him so as to intimidate the men." If indiscriminate mobility were to be encouraged, unionists might be quite as much of a menace as nonunionists.

The original leaders, sceptical of a job monopoly held by "laborers," had not troubled much about this. Mobile men, like the builders, and perhaps the expanding and far from crystallized Midland semi-skilled engineering workers, might maintain the old view. (Hence the support of the London district of the Gas-workers, and perhaps the spokesmen of the Workers' Union for the old slogan in 1911–1914.) Revolutionaries who thought in terms of class militancy would detect the "reformist" danger in restrictionism and champion the one big union, as Larkin and Connolly did. Yet, in fact, it was clear by 1910–1914 that the union of all "unskilled" workers, however desirable, would not be one of a mass of individual floating laborers, but one of a great many local job monopolies and closed shops, whose special interests had to be safeguarded, if they were to give up their independence. The extremely significant unity discussions between the General Labourers' National Council and the Transport Workers' Federation in 1911–1914 reached deadlock on this very point. It was only some ten years later, when the Dockers' Union (largely on the model of Bevin's Bristol organization) had evolved a scheme of autonomy for trade groups, that the vast mergers which gave birth to the Transport and General and General and Municipal Workers became possible. (However, the adoption of a more flexible organization was merely a condition of their success; the power which propelled separate unions towards amalgamation was largely political and revolutionary unrest.)

We can thus distinguish three stages in general union tactics: the old-fashioned general unionism of 1889–1892; the cautious, limited and conservative "sectional" unionism of 1892–1910; and the revolutionary urge for amalgamation, the industrial unionism or the articulated "general" organization of the modern Transport Workers, which arose out of the expansions of 1911–1920. Both the first and the third aimed at the organization of all "unskilled" workers. The second—chiefly under the pressure of circumstance—renounced it in practice, confining itself to the organization of those groups capable of old-fashioned bargaining. It is significant, for example, that it utterly failed to organize the genuinely weak—e.g., the women. In spite of its early enthusiasm for women's organization, the 32,000 members of Gas-workers in 1908 contained only some 800 women. General unionism in this period between the expansions had indeed become something like the sectional unionism of certain "unskilled" groups in the American Federation of Labor between 1896 and 1935; the Teamsters, the Hod-Carriers, etc. Had there been no second expansion within twenty years of the first, it might well have been assimilated to the craft-pattern, as in the USA.

The "new unionism" of 1889 thus became uncomfortably like the "old unionism" it had once fought; and the politics of its leaders changed accordingly. The revolutionary Marxists who led the Dockers and Gas-workers then, were increasingly replaced by much milder socialists (though for auld lang syne some of them continued to call themselves Marxian Social Democrats). Ernest Bevin, not Tom Mann, was to dominate the Dockers after their second expansion. The Gas-workers, a very markedly "party-dominated" organization, whose leader was a protégé of Engels, whose *éminences grises* in the early 1890s were the Marx-Avelings, and most of whose key positions were held by Social Democrats, became the union of the Rt. Hon. J. R. Clynes, and a distinctly moderate body.

Yet after 1906 the fall in real wages and the rank-and-file unrest forced unions once again on to the offensive. The problems of massive recruitment and aggressive bargaining obliged leaders to reconsider their tactics. Hitherto this had not been really necessary. The impetus of the expansion of 1889 had given them all the offensive strength they originally needed. When slump and employers' attacks had weeded out all but the strongest, the general unions had discovered powerful defensive resources which enabled them to survive. They spread their risks between industries and areas not all of which were liable to attack at the same time. They acted, in fact, as a convenient "banker" for a multiplicity of local and sectional bargaining units. Such spreading of risks was quite essential, for the "laborers' " union faced actuarially quite unpredictable risks: at any moment its funds might be drained by disputes between masters and "artisans," or between skilled unions. Hence nothing would have been gained, had the NAUL turned itself into a pure shipyard union, or the Dockers split up into separate waterside and tinplate trade societies. On the contrary; the incentive to recruit widely remained. Thus the Gas-workers took in the pit-top men they had originally refused, and the three main general unions used the boom of 1898–1900 to make important conquests—their only really solid advances between the two expansions—into coal, iron, steel and tinplate in South Wales, and the Nottingham-Derby-South Yorkshire area. If much of the membership fluctuated, that need not weaken the union provided it had a nucleus of regular branches. On the contrary, a steady influx of entrance fees and temporary subscriptions merely added to the funds of societies which could not charge the high dues of the craft unions.

The more acute left-wingers, however, had long recognized the need for a more adequate aggressive tactic. Even in the 1889 days all manner of federations and centralized "general staffs" had been suggested. Tom Mann, incomparably the ablest of the radicals, had even used the small expansion of 1898–1900 to found a body halfway between "general" and "industrial" unions, the Workers' Union, which was to embrace all industries and grades of skill, including the highest. This union was not very successful until after 1911, when it became one of the major general unions, and one which long retained certain ecumenical ambitions. Mann's theories did, however, enable it to make exceptional headway among farm-laborers, and in the mass-production engineering of the Midlands, where the coordinating of various degrees of skill was urgent, and the national craft unions relatively weak. From 1906, however, other unions—again largely under the impulse of the Left—awoke to the importance of "strategic" recruiting, and systematic all-grades bargaining. Certainly by 1911 the Bristol dockers were systematically recruiting strategically important grades, and the Dockers' Union as a whole took up the cause of "industrial unionism" and the new Transport Workers' Federation with enthusiasm.

For most general unions, however, the problem of "industrial" bargaining resolved itself not so much into one of forming bodies covering an entire industry, but into one of recruitment, of demarcation, and of unscrambling their eggs. Recruitment was easy, at any rate in times of expansion. Demarcation was more difficult, for they naturally cut across whatever industrial boundaries could be drawn. It was indeed on this rock that systematic unionism eventually foundered in the 1920s. However, certain local arrangements had long been made—the Bristol dockers promised not to poach galvanizers, the Gas-workers refraining from coal-porters—and wide federations like the Transport Workers' were some help. But within each union the trades formed a jumbled mass; unless, as happened sometimes, a particular district was predominantly composed of men in one industry, and could thus form a de facto "trade section." NAUL thus had its geographically distinct waterside and ship-repairing groups, the Dockers their tinplate district, the Gas-workers their dyers, etc. Yet that was not enough. As early as 1893 the gas-workers in the Gas-workers' Union had wanted to federate with the miners, with whom their strategic interests lay; as the Coal-porters' Union had done. But the dyers and chemical workers in the union objected strongly to paying out affiliation fees for what was quite irrelevant to them, and the matter was shelved. So long as the old indiscriminate organization existed, trades would inevitably get in each other's way.

As the unions grew after 1906, and above all as they took in non-localized industries, they thus had to develop greater flexibility. The Dockers took the lead in this, no doubt because the two strongly marked and contrasting units of Bristol waterside and Welsh tinplate workers, which dominated the union, forced them to grant each considerable autonomy. In 1911–1914 we can see the seeds of the new model sprouting in the west: the "Tinplate District" was converted into a trade section, to be a pattern for others, and, an even greater break, a "galvanizing section" was set up on a mainly non-geographical basis. The Transport and General Workers' Union was later to be built on systematic trade autonomy. It had its reward. In 1910 the Dockers were, speaking nationally, one of the least successful, and by no means the largest of the general unions. In the course of the next twenty years they were to overhaul the less systematically organized Gas-workers, to become the largest union in the country. But, whether the adoption of trade autonomy was systematic or not, all general unions moved in the same direction. By the time of the great amalgamations after World War I, they were on their way to becoming alliances of trade and industrial sections, rather than, in the past, of local bargaining units. It is as such that they function today.

Arthur Mitzman
SIT-IN STRIKES IN FRANCE (1936–1937)

Arthur Mitzman teaches at Simon Fraser University in Burnaby, B.C., Canada. His work in labor history has been limited, but insightful. More recently, he has turned his attention to intellectual history and produced a thought-provoking study of Max Weber. In an article on the French workers' reaction to the Popular Front government—a left-wing cabinet headed by a Social-ist, Leon Blum—Mitzman asked why the workers, who had welcomed the government joyously in 1936, watched its fall from power indifferently in 1937? He refutes the traditional answer that the Communist party manipulated the change, and asserts that the workers themselves became disillusioned, and the Communist party simply fell into line. The workers had expressed their initial hopes in a "massive, spontaneous" wave of sit-down strikes, which had produced concessions such as collective negotiations and pay raises. Within months, they had to defend their gains by sit-in strikes with little assistance from the government. The following excerpt describes and explains the latter strikes, and the first futile efforts at compulsory arbitration in France.

The greatest strike wave France had ever experienced reached its crest in the second week of June, 1936, when over a million men downed their tools. Thereafter, the major demands of the strikers having been satisfied, strikes slowly subsided. By the third week of July, all but 33,000 people had returned to work, and on August 17 and 18, for the first time since May, *Le Temps* failed to print a line of strike news. This calm was quickly broken by a new surge of unrest that had little of the peaceful character of the earlier sit-down strikes and seemed to be caused as much by employer intransigence as by a rapidly rising cost of living.

On August 19, one of the first strikes reported after the mid-August hiatus was a strike of government workers. This was a particularly bad omen for the Blum regime. The Civil Servants' Federation had always been noted for its *lack* of the endemic *incivisme* which made so many Frenchmen view their government as an independent predator rather than an embodiment of the public interest. And of all the trade union groups, the civil servants were considered

From Arthur Mitzman, "The French Working Class and the Blum Government," in the *International Review of Social History*, vol. 9, part 3 (1964), pp. 363–389. Reprinted by permission of the International Institute for Social History, Amsterdam. Footnotes omitted.

closest to the Socialists. Indeed, according to André Delmas, the *fonctionnaires* were "the elements on which [Blum] counted on being able to support himself with most security." If this was all Blum could expect from his friends, what must his enemies be preparing!

The plans of Blum's enemies in the reorganized employers' federation soon became clear. Through a resolute campaign of resistance to organized labor, the new *Confédération Générale du Patronat Français*, was determined to prevent any new gains by labor and to take back as many of the concessions granted at Matignon[1] as possible. One of the most anti-union of the employers' subgroups, because of the nineteenth-century paternalism of most of its members, was the textile employers' federation. This group was even more eager to recoup the losses of June than the CGPF, which it had left in disgust after Matignon and refused to rejoin. Thus, the strikes of late summer and early fall, 1936, had four principal characteristics. A great many of them took place in textile mills, which were concentrated in the north of France. They were frequently touched off by dismissals of union workers, and the fear of lockouts. They were aggravated, where not actually caused, by sharp rises in the cost of living. They were usually prolonged by the refusal of the employers—especially the textile employers—to negotiate until their workers left company property.

On August 19 and 20, this new pattern began to appear with strikes in the Nord and other departments over dismissals and layoffs of workers. On August 22 another strike in the Nord, at Lille, developed over the employment of nonunion labor: on the twenty-fourth, a sympathy strike was declared in nearby Roubaix and Tourcoing. All three of these cities were major textile centers. The festive mood of the June strikes was absent: at least one case occurred where strikers went to the home of a nonstriking worker and destroyed property.

On August 25, the Talbot factory locked out 1,000 workers in the Paris area, claiming it could not meet the new wage rates. The workers countered that orders were plentiful and that the only reason for the lockout was to exert pressure on the government to obtain credits. More lockouts were feared. On August 29, 1,100 men

---

[1] In the Matignon agreements of 1936, the Blum government got representatives of employers to recognize collective bargaining, pay raises of 7 to 15 percent, workers' delegates in factories, the forty-hour week, and so on.—Ed.

occupied a plant in Belfort. On August 30, more strikes, especially in the Nord, over dismissals of union members, were reported. On August 31, 5,000 coal miners of the northern region left their pits.

The pace of the new strike wave accelerated almost daily. On September 3, 1,800 weavers sat down in their plants at Amiens, while strikes for higher wages involved 1,400 men in Soissons. [September] 4 saw 6,000 metallurgy workers leave their jobs in Grenoble. The next day, presumably under the pressure of their employers' refusal to negotiate, the weavers of Amiens agreed to leave their plants for the duration of the strike. In the following four days, a rash of strikes by dockers and shipyard workers broke out in La Seyne, Cherbourg, and La Rochelle. On the tenth of September, 10,000 metallurgy workers in the Nord struck for wage increases to keep up with the cost of living. On the eleventh, 30,000 textile workers locked themselves into their factories in Lille.

Two days later, the Lille strikers, under government pressure, agreed to evacuate their plants, only to reoccupy them on the fourteenth after their employers broke off negotiations. On the seventeenth, 24,000 textile workers in the Vosges struck, while the Lille strike continued. After an attempt at government arbitration failed because of the employers' refusal to cooperate with the government, the strike in Lille was settled by a compromise on the nineteenth. On the same day, the Hotchkiss workers in Clichy walked out because of feared dismissals, and returned only when assured they would not take place.

The next day, September 20, *Le Temps* reported major strikes in progress at Douai and Marseilles in metallurgy, and at Amiens, in the Vosges, and at Lyons, in textiles. On the twenty-first, textile workers in Roubaix and Tourcoing prepared to strike, while a small textile plant in Lille, employing 70 men, closed down because it could not afford to pay new wage rates. The Roubaix-Tourcoing strike was avoided, but on the twenty-fourth, the epidemic of metal workers' walkouts reached Paris, and sent men out by the tens of thousands. The strikes of textile workers in Vosges and Lyons remained unsettled, and, on the twenty-sixth of September, a special meeting of the CGT's[2] national committee was called to review the situation.

---

[2] CGT stands for the Confédération Général du Travail, the non-Communist trade union congress.—Ed.

In his speech before this body, Jouhaux[3] condemned both the provocations of the employers and the inexperience of the workers and ended with an important new list of demands for government intervention to control the situation. He condemned the press reaction to the strikes, asserting that ". . . every move of the workers is savagely exploited to create an atmosphere of panic from which our adversaries hope to gain profit." He admitted the unreasoning impulsiveness of the great mass of newly unionized workers, who wanted "immediately, full satisfaction for all their demands," and denounced "troublemaking elements inside each factory," who used this impulsiveness. His conclusion was that it was necessary to "develop in the masses a sense of discipline," which could only be done "by guaranteeing all the acquired rights." To obtain such a guarantee, Jouhaux made three demands: (1) That factories be closed by the government during strikes so that neither workers nor management could get into them; (2) That a mobile scale be established for workers' wages, to keep pace with the cost of living; (3) That a system of compulsory arbitration be established by the government for handling labor disputes. All three of these points were in marked contradiction to the CGT's traditional stand against government regulation. But with a friendly government, and an unfriendly management which, as the Lille strike showed, was obviously not amenable to any voluntary procedures, the CGT realized it had more to gain than to lose by its proposals.

Neutralization of struck factories would have virtually ended all need for sit-down strikes by removing their most important cause: the workers' fear that struck factories would be run by strikebreakers. Neutralization, however, was bitterly opposed by all employers, and this position, probably coupled with the French public's traditional mistrust of government authority, prevented the measure from even being proposed under the Blum regime. The mobile wage scale was proposed by Blum a few days after the CGT conference, as part of the devaluation law, but it was quickly rejected. This left only conciliation and arbitration as possible means of holding down labor conflicts. Though the *Chambre* was willing to grant Blum rather broad powers to safeguard purchasing power, including an arbitration system, the Senate rejected these on the grounds that no special powers should be given until future events showed their

[3] Jouhaux was Secretary General of the CGT.—Ed.

necessity. Blum was finally able to obtain only the authority to establish compulsory arbitration for wage claims arising out of price increases.

This was obviously insufficient, since many strikes had dismissals of union members as their cause. Summing up a good part of the basis for the strike record of September, 1936, *La Voix du peuple,* monthly CGT organ, complained of "numerous cases of violation of social legislation and of failure to respect the free exercise of union rights. An offensive has been unleashed by certain employers' circles to take back all or part of the advantages granted the workers." The CGT then went on to repeat its proposals for a conciliation and arbitration system for all industrial disputes. However, there was little hope that the employers could be brought into a voluntary agreement with labor on such a system: "These propositions have not encountered . . . a very sympathetic response in employers' circles. . . . The CGPF has recently placed at its head new men whose presence at this post, if one can judge by what one knows of them, does not appear likely to facilitate things."

This proved to be an accurate forecast of what was to happen to Blum's efforts to obtain agreement from the employers on a voluntary system. Negotiations between CGT, CGPF and government representatives started in mid-September and dragged on for ten weeks until, in late November, the employers' delegation walked out for good and Blum was forced to apply to the Assembly for a comprehensive compulsory arbitration bill.

During these months, strike activity, though generally less than a tenth what it had been in June, continued at a very high level. In the last third of 1936, more strikes (2,428) occurred than in any previous year of French history, while the number of strikers (295,000) exceeded that of any year since 1930. Prices rose unceasingly, and with them, the cost of living. The actual increase in weekly wages resulting from the June strikes had been about 17 percent. But the September retail price indices revealed a 6 percent increase in the cost of living over May, the November ones, a 13.5 percent increase. Speaking of the strikes in this period, Joel Colton states, "Had there been no other contributory causes, the rise in prices alone would have been sufficient cause for labor unrest." It may well have occurred to the workers that what the Popular Front regime had given them in human dignity and a higher standard of living, union-busting employers and rising prices were taking away. In the case of Spain, they had seen that, though Blum's heart may have been in the right place, his foreign policy was anchored in the Thames, and that consequently he could do no more for their unfortunate Spanish brothers than English Toryism would allow him —which was nothing at all. The failure of their government to defend the gains of June was even more galling, since these were, after all, *their* rights and *their* wages that were being slowly eroded. The pressure was clearly on Blum to rectify the situation. Not only was he losing vital political support, but his whole social and economic policy, built as it was around the idea of inducing economic recovery through increased purchasing power, was in jeopardy. But all Blum could do for the workers was to push compulsory arbitration through the Senate and, as we shall see, this was far from enough.

The creaky mechanism of the arbitration law that was passed on the last day of 1936, can best be understood in its actual functioning. As an example of this functioning, arbitration in the Paris metal industry reveals the experience of a large and significant group of workers.

The Paris metallurgical union had grown from a membership of about 10,000 before the strike to 200,000 afterward. The old CGT militants were overwhelmed by swarms of impatient new recruits who, for the reasons outlined above, were almost all Communist sympathizers. For years prior to the strike of May–June, 1936, the metal workers' union had attempted to enter negotiations with the industry's employers' association. All those attempts had failed because of the employers' refusal to even discuss with the union. Relations between workers and management showed no improvement in the post-strike period. Throughout the latter months of 1936, their employers made numerous, though largely unsuccessful, attempts to secure a delay in the date for enacting the forty-hour week, attempts which were probably known and resented by the workers. At the same time, the price rise in the Paris area was nullifying their gains of the summer. As a result of the price rise, the long tradition of anti-unionism on the employers' part and the recent September metal strikes, relations between management and workers were a mixture of resentment and mistrust. In November,

1936, the metal workers reacted vigorously to the destruction of their newly acquired purchasing power by demanding a 15 percent wage increase. When it was refused, the union threatened a strike, but, realizing that compulsory arbitration would soon be passed, refrained from any more than token stoppages.

In early January the metal union submitted its demands to arbitration. The man appointed by the government to reach a decision was Professor William Oualid, a scholar known for his labor sympathies. On February 7, 1937, Professor Oualid handed down his decision. While granting the union's claim that there had been a 15 percent increase in the cost of living between May and December, 1936, he allowed a wage increase of only 8.5 percent, less than three-fifths of the price rise. In doing so, he pointed out that granting full compensation for the higher prices would only encourage further price inflation, and so produce more harm for the national economy than good for the workers.

The union protested vehemently against this decision, particularly since there had been a further rise in the cost of living of 5 percent between its original demand and the arbitration decision. As a result of its agitation, another arbitration award was granted the metal workers in March, 1937, which brought the total increase over May in weekly wages to between 12.5 percent for the highest and 15.2 percent for the lowest paid category of workers. But by March the cost of living had risen 20.2 percent over May, leaving the Paris unionists, after ten months of *Front Populaire* government, with barely two-thirds of the increased purchasing power they had won for themselves in June.

A sense of mistrust in their employer's good faith had already been instilled in the workers by the persistent attempts of the Union of Metal Industries to obtain a legal delay in the application of the forty-hour week. Now the government proved a disappointment —small wonder that the workers were no longer willing to support it with militant action. Far from being an especially bad case, the experience of the Paris metal union was probably better than average. Indeed, Joel Colton maintains that "it exploited the arbitration system to the maximum and extracted all possible benefits from it. . . ." Summarizing the operation of the 1936 Arbitration Act, Colton says,

> *the arbitrators had tried to hold the line against a runaway wage-price spiral, granting only a partial wage adjustment to cost of living rises,*

rarely granting complete retroactivity and refusing unanimously to grant automatic sliding wage scales for the future. Their decisions represented a denial, past, present, and future, of total wage compensation for the increased living costs. . . . There is no doubt that the excessive caution of the arbitrators and a consuming concern for preventing inflation resulted in many instances of injustice to labor. . . . (*My emphasis, A.M.*)

Colton adds that, from the point of view of the national economy, it could be argued that none of the wage increases were justified, since they encouraged inflation; but this statement in no way vitiates the significance of his assertion that "many instances of injustice to labor" resulted. From the standpoint of the French worker, and from my own standpoint in trying to understand the change in the workers' attitude towards the Blum regime, the crucial fact is that arbitration under a Socialist premier did not grant anything like the full compensation for price increases that the workers expected.

In the *Economist* for February 13, 1937, a report from France described the public's reaction to rising prices in the following terms:

"What is the increase in wages worth if it is absorbed at once by the rise in prices" is the slogan invariably heard in the streets, when a further increase in the price of bread, or wine, or butter occurs. The Popular Front is anxious, and the organs of the Left demand that the rise in prices should be checked at once. The leaders of the Trade Unions are urging their followers to be patient, to "digest" the labor reforms and to safeguard the victory of the Popular Front. But their patience will not last for long.

The events of the next four weeks were to stretch this patience to the limit and finally to snap it. On the one hand, the government's supporters were urging new reforms which would cost billions of francs; a national unemployment fund; old-age pensions for workers; relief for the farmers (whose prices had been fixed before the general price rises); wage increases for civil servants. On the other hand, M. Caillaux had warned that the Senate finance committee would not certify any new expenditures unless accompanied by economies in other areas; the investing public was boycotting government bonds; and Blum seemed ready to try halting the price rises by lowering import duties, which would occasion an inevitable drain on the Exchange Equalization Fund, and so cause the government more financial embarrassment.

In mid-February, 1937, Blum appealed to the men of the Left for a breathing space. But in their eyes, practically everything the government had done since the summer was a breathing space. Thus, union leaders partial to the CGT Plan, who had been quiet since the 1936 elections in order to give Blum's social and economic policies a chance to work, now became increasingly vocal; in doing so, they probably reflected and certainly stimulated the growing disaffection of their troops from the government.

The more radical voice of labor in the weeks from mid-February to early March undid Blum's efforts to gain the confidence of banking and business interests. The consequent precariousness of his financial situation was driving Blum to a complete repudiation of his social and economic policy. But this policy, after Blum had renounced any possibility of aiding republican Spain, and internal fascism had proven to be a paper dragon, was the sole remaining bond between the government and the proletariat. When, on March fifth, Blum finally gave in completely to conservative demands for an orthodox economic policy (by dropping his government's public works program and giving control of the Exchange Stabilization Fund to financial conservatives), he created an irreparable breach between himself and the workers who, for all their suspicions, had hoped for so much from the Socialist premier. The *Economist* astutely noted this breach when it commented that the great result of the policy change was the shock created in the ranks of the Popular Front, and added that "if the Blum cabinet falls, a successor may come without riots in the street. In that sense," it concluded, "the danger of a revolution is past."

Ten days later, in the Parisian workers' suburb of Clichy, street riots did occur. But far from being in defense of the Blum regime, they constituted a bloody proletarian outbreak against it.

II POLITICAL MILITANCY, 1834-1939

Asa Briggs

CHARTISM'S GEOGRAPHIC AND ECONOMIC DIVISIONS

Asa Briggs, presently vice chancellor of the University of Sussex, England, has written on topics so various as broadcasting and labor, cities and Chartism. Much of his work has been on the Victorian period in England; and much of it has drawn on local history. In the following excerpt, he brings his extensive knowledge of the Victorian period and of local history to bear upon the findings of a number of grass-roots studies of the Chartist movement. The movement took its name from the Charter, a document that demanded six political reforms, including universal male suffrage. The Charter was formulated in 1838 by a group of London radicals, who promptly began a petition campaign for it. The campaign blossomed into demonstrations that were to last, on and off, for a decade. This movement is usually seen as a national one, divided over tactics at the leadership level. Briggs disagrees: he believes the divisions go much deeper, into the geographic, professional and economic divisions of the Chartist rank and file.

The pull of early Chartism seems to have been strongest in two kinds of place—first, in old centers of decaying or contracting industry, like Trowbridge in Wiltshire or Carmarthen in Wales, and second, in the new or expanding single-industry towns like Stockport, described by Engels as "one of the darkest and smokiest holes in the whole industrial area." Big cities, which served as regional capitals, had large numbers of Chartists, but were sometimes less militant than adjacent industrial areas. Manchester and Birmingham, for example, were less active in the middle years of Chartism than the textile and metal-working districts nearby: Leeds was quieter than Halifax. In the big cities, where political radicalism had established itself long before the drafting of the Charter, there were more attempts at political accommodation between Chartists and other reformers, although most of them were unsuccessful. Chartism was not strong—and in some cases it was almost nonexistent— in completely agricultural villages, those of Kent or Dorset, for example, in old market towns like Ripon or Bedford, and in new industrial centers with a mixed economy, like St. Helens.

From Asa Briggs, "The Local Background of Chartism," in *Chartist Studies*, ed. Asa Briggs (London, 1959), pp. 3–15. Reprinted by permission of Macmillan London and Basingstoke, and St. Martin's Press. Footnotes omitted.

Such differences in appeal cannot be attributed to the accident of the presence or absence of active Chartist personalities, however significant was the influence of personality in particular cases. Nor can they be evaluated, however, within a framework of geographical determinism. It is dangerous to personify Manchester and Birmingham or to rely on broad generalizations about North and South or London and the provinces. Local differences need to be related to economic and social structure—to the composition of the labor force, the conditions of work, including relations between "masters" and "men," and the timing and extent of local unemployment. Other social factors, including the influence of religion, may also be relevant. In many places Nonconformity figures prominently in the local Chartist story.

There were three main groups within the heterogeneous labor force which played a special part in the development of Chartism—a section of the superior craftsmen, including printers, cobblers, tailors, cabinetmakers, booksellers and small shopkeepers; factory operatives, concentrated in the textiles districts, and familiarly referred to in the current vulgar political economy of the times as "hands"; and domestic outworkers, including not only handloom weavers but such producers as framework knitters and nailmakers. The economic interests and fortunes of these three groups were not always the same. W. T. Thornton, the economist, remarked in 1846 that "the laboring population has . . . been spoken of as if it formed only one class, but it is really divided into several, among which the rates of remuneration are far from being uniform . . . so that, in order to represent with perfect fidelity the state of the laboring population, it would be necessary to describe each class separately." It was not only rates of remuneration which diverged, but the extent of social security, regularity of earnings, the climate of industrial relations, status in the local community, and prospects of future advancement, both for the individual and for members of the family.

A main theme in Chartist history was the attempt to create a sense of class unity which would bind together these three groups. The attempt was never completely successful, however, and differences not only between one Chartist "locality" and another but within Chartist "localities" can be explained in part by differences in the balance of the three groups.

Not all the superior craftsmen were drawn into Chartism. New-style craftsmen, like machine-builders, for example, were never prominent. On the other hand, a minority of superior craftsmen, those described by William Lovett and the London Working Men's Association as "the *intelligent* and *influential* portion of the working classes in town and country," were the leaven of the early Chartist movement, and many of them remained faithful to it until the end. Their belief in the Six Points of the Charter was not conditioned by the movements of the trade cycle, and many of them had been converted to belief in reform—if they needed to be converted—before the Charter was drafted. Although the most articulate of them often misunderstood those of their "fellow workmen" who "croaked over their grievances with maudlin brains" and were themselves misunderstood by those militant operatives who dismissed them as "a middle-class set of agitators," they sought to foster a "union of sentiment" among the working classes, "which is essential to the prosecution of any great object." They refused to look to "great men" or to "idols" and endeavored to create working-class "discrimination and independent spirit in the management of their political affairs." Scattered about the country, they were the pillars of the Working Men's Associations. They included men like Henry Lovewell, the Ipswich journeyman tailor who already possessed the franchise in 1837 and had been a foundation member of the Mechanics Institute. Their very respectability, often associated with Nonconformity, which served as an asset to them in dealing with the "middle classes," usually hindered them in dealing with "fustian jackets, unshorn chins and blistered hands."

The factory operatives were concentrated in particular parts of the country—Lancashire, described by Engels as "the mainspring of all the workers' movements," the scene of the great industrial transformation of the late eighteenth and early nineteenth centuries, "the cotton kingdom," the West Riding of Yorkshire, where the woollen industry was in course of transformation, in what Faucher called "a regime of transition" between old and new methods of production; parts of Cumberland, Derbyshire, Wales and the West of England; and West Scotland. In 1839 there were 192 cotton mills in Scotland employing 31,000 workers. All but 17 of these were located in Lanark and Renfrew. There was a further concentration within these counties as there was in Lancashire and the West Riding.

Work in factories entailed a new discipline and enforced subordination, but it also stimulated an enhanced sense of solidarity and a quest for social and political independence. In the words of Ernest Jones, who wrote vigorously and eloquently about the implications of steam power:

> *Up in factory! Up in mill!*
> *Freedom's mighty phalanx swell . . .*
> *Fear ye not your masters' power;*
> *Men are strong when men unite . . .*
> *And flowers will grow in blooming-time,*
> *Where prison-doors their jarring cease:*
> *For liberty will banish crime—*
> Contentment *is the best* Police.

Both the myth of a pre-factory golden age and the dream of a new social order in the future influenced the thinking—and, equally important, the feeling—of the factory operatives, while both their means of action and their objectives shifted during the course of the 1830s and 1840s. The pendulum swung between economic action through the trade unions and political action through Chartism. "Good times" favored the former; "bad times" the latter. The rhythms of what the Leeds Socialist John Francis Bray called "inordinate idleness and incessant toil" influenced the timing and the intensity of all forms of organization. At different times "the equalization of wages" through "general union," the Six Points of the Charter, the battle for the Ten Hours' working day, the slogan of "a fair day's wages for a fair day's work," turn-outs and plug drawing, the repeal of the corn laws, and O'Connor's Land Plan[1] appealed to all or some groups of factory operatives. The Charter was thus one objective among several, and the extent to which it figured as the main objective depended not only on the forcefulness and skill of Chartist leadership but on the state of the domestic and overseas market for textile goods. Some factory operatives re-

---

[1] Turn-outs and plug-drawing were methods of closing down factories for a strike in the 1830s and 1840s. The corn laws protected agriculture and in the 1830s and 1840s were being attacked by the Anti-Corn Law League. O'Connor was a Chartist leader who took up an abortive scheme to return workers to the land in the 1840s. —Ed.

mained faithful to Chartism through all its vicissitudes, but the crowds ebbed and flowed with the economic tides.

The absence of a factory system not only in London but in Birmingham is important in explaining local differences. In Birmingham the most important economic unit was not the factory, but the small workshop, and within the workshop small masters rather than industrial capitalists worked in close contact with skilled artisans. Economic development in Birmingham in the first half of the nineteenth century multiplied the number of producing units rather than added to the scale of existing enterprise. Labor-saving machinery, driven by steam power, was far less important than in Manchester. "The operation of mechanism in this town," wrote a Birmingham man in 1836, "is to effect that alone, which requires more *force* than the *arm* and the tools of the workman could yield, still leaving his skill and experience of head, hand and eye in full exercise; so that Birmingham has suffered infinitely less from the introduction of machinery than those towns where it is in marked degree, an actual substitute for human labor." Another feature of Birmingham society was marked social mobility which blurred sharp class distinctions. Small masters might fail in their enterprises and become journeymen again: journeymen had chances of rising when times were good. "It is easy to see," Faucher said of the city, "that the *bourgeoisie,* which in all urban centers is the basis of society, scarcely rises in Birmingham above the inferior groups in society." Engels and Cobden were agreed about the political consequences of this social system, and Engels quoted Faucher's phrase "industrial democracy" and described the city as "Radical rather than Chartist." In fact, as we shall see, Birmingham played an important part in the birth of the Chartist movement as an organized national force, although it had lost much of its importance by the time that Engels wrote.

The third labor group, which was generally recognized by contemporaries to be a key group in Chartist politics, consisted of domestic outworkers. In the Black Country, adjacent to Birmingham, there were large numbers of nailmakers living near the starvation level. In Lancashire, the West Riding of Yorkshire, the West Country, Wales and Scotland there were handloom weavers fighting a grim losing battle against the machine. In the West Midlands there were framework knitters employed in an over-stocked occupation where there was not enough work to go round. It was because all other attempts at betterment broke down that most of these outworkers turned towards Chartism. Many of them had had the reputation in the 1820s of being a quiet, hard-working, nonpolitical section of the population, and certainly their first reaction to the privation and distress which followed the end of the Napoleonic Wars was to appeal to the local justices of the peace and to the government for economic protection. The failure of this appeal, which ran counter to the interests of factory owners and the ideas of the newly powerful political economists, led them direct into politics along a road of despair. How little they could expect to get from government was clearly brought out in the *Report of the Royal Commission on Handloom Weavers,* appointed in 1838 "to report whether any, and, if so, what measures could be devised for their relief." Nassau Senior, the economist, was the chief draftsman of the report, which has recently been described as an "admirable" exercise in economic logic. "The power of the Czar of Russia," the Commissioners concluded,

> *could not raise the wages of men so situate. He might indeed order a scale of prices to be paid them for the work which they did, but in such cases the manufacturer would soon cease to give out work, as it would be against his interest to do it. The Czar of Russia, either by fixing on a high scale of wages, or by a direct command, might put an end to the occupation altogether, and such would be a most merciful exercise of his unlimited power; but the authority of the Government of a free country cannot thus control the subjects even for their own good; and all that remains, therefore, is to enlighten the handloom weavers as to their real situation, warn them to flee from the trade, and to beware of leading their children into it, as they would beware of the commission of the most atrocious of crimes.*

Such advice, backed up as it was by economic as well as political authority, in considerable measure justifies Thomas Carlyle's emphasis on "lack of due guidance" besides lack of food and shelter as the cause of the growth of the *isms* of his age. And long before the Commissioners reported nationally, handloom weavers had been told locally that their request for public help was "absolute folly," "founded in utter ignorance of the circumstances which regulate the wages of labor which it is impossible for Parliament to control." It is not surprising that after suffering severely even when times were "good," the weavers looked when times were bad not to the authority of a Czar of Russia but to the authority of local and national Chartist leaders. The leaders they preferred were those who knew how to use and were willing to use militant headstrong language, who painted bright pictures of the past—a past which had certainly provided handloom weavers not only with bigger wages but with an assured and recognized position in society—and who related the political demand for universal suffrage to the demand for food and shelter. The language of hunger was common to all those parts of the country where outworkers were concentrated. In Lancashire J. R. Stephens defined universal suffrage as the means to secure every working man's "right" to a good coat on his back, a good roof over his head and a good dinner on his table. In the West Riding Richard Oastler, who never committed himself to support of the Chartist political program, attacked the factory system as a "slaughterhouse system" and added that he did not "think that the Government can claim on any ground the allegiance of the operatives when they see that capital and property are protected and their labor is left to chance." In the East Midlands, the editor of the *Leicester Chronicle* declared that, since the framework knitters could not hope to achieve genuine social independence, it was not surprising that they turned to a social Chartism, which offered the prospect of "better wages, limited hours of labor, comfort, independence, happiness . . . all that the fond heart of suffering man pictures to him of joy and prosperity in his happiest moments." In Wiltshire, a Trowbridge Chartist put the matter even more plainly. He promised his audience "plenty of roast beef, plum pudding and strong beer by working three hours a day."

There is a wide gap between language of this kind and the more sophisticated language of skilled artisans and craftsmen. It was the strength of O'Connor that he knew how to talk effectively to despairing domestic workers who were more interested during 1837 in the threat of the New Poor Law of 1834[2] than in political panaceas. The Poor Law Commissioners turned their attention in January 1837 to the industrial districts which hitherto they had left alone. They had met with some earlier resistance in the South—in Suf-

---

[2] The New Poor Law of 1834 insisted that ablebodied poor receive relief only in the workhouse, where they would, among other things, be separated from their families. —Ed.

folk, for instance, and in small market towns like Bishop's Stortford and Saffron Walden—but in the north they were welcomed with what J. R. Stephens called "the tocsin of revolt." Oastler, the revered local leader, and O'Connor, who was beginning to fascinate angry audiences everywhere, both addressed a mass meeting in Huddersfield one week after the arrival of Alfred Power, the Assistant Poor Law Commissioner; it was Oastler who coined the phrase of the moment: "Damnation, eternal damnation to the fiend-begotten, coarser-food New Poor Law," the title he gave to the pamphlet version of his speech. O'Connor was shrewd enough to encourage the proliferation of grievances rather than to canalize them. Later on he told Lovett in 1842, "I don't lead; I am driven by the people. The people gave the lead to the agitation and we followed." The *Northern Star,* the first number of which appeared in Leeds on 18 November 1837, reported all local protest meetings with equal enthusiasm. It was not until the winter of 1837–1838 that O'Connor turned decisively to the suffrage agitation, and it was not until the spring of 1838, on the eve of the drafting of the Charter, that the Anti-Poor Law movement was merged into the political agitation for parliamentary reform.

Before examining in more detail the sequence of events which led to the extended nation-wide campaign, three features of the Anti-Poor Law movement need to be set in their place, and the relationship between Chartism and trade-unionism needs to be more fully considered.

The fact that the Poor Law Commissioners set out to put the 1834 Act into operation in the North of England just at the moment that business depression was leading to unemployment of factory operatives as well as starvation among the handloom weavers created the broadest possible front of local opposition. The Act had been intended not to solve the problems of an industrial society but to establish a free labor market in the pauperized agricultural counties. In the north a free labor market already existed. The principle of less eligibility, the cornerstone of the 1834 Act, had no relevance to conditions of involuntary mass industrial unemployment. The attempt to herd together inside the workhouses those people in receipt of poor relief was pointless as well as dangerous. "It imposed a disgraceful stigma on the genuinely unemployed and their families, it was actually far more costly than out-relief, and finally it was tantamount to waging social war." The language of the opponents of the Act was as violent as any of the later language employed by the militant Chartists. The workhouses were universally known as "Bastilles," orders were given by local leaders to destroy them, rioting was widespread, and memories of resistance influenced not only Chartist history but the later history of working-class movements in the nineteenth century. The attempt to apply the New Poor Law "did more to sour the hearts of the laboring population than did the privations consequent on all the actual poverty of the land."

Before the Anti-Poor Law movement could merge into Chartism it had to shed many of its "Tory" sympathizers, men who hated "centralization," looked to the restoration of an old form of society, deemed "Whiggery" and "the march of improvement" as the real curses of the country, and far from wanting further parliamentary reform intensely disliked the measure of "middle-class" reform which had been passed in 1832. In August 1837 the Whig whip E. J. Stanley wrote to Edwin Chadwick, the most fervent and logical advocate of the principles of 1834, that "North of Trent the law is as unpopular as it is possible with all classes—Justices and Guardians for political purposes—overseers, now discontinued, from interested motives. . . . The whole of the manufacturing population vehemently against it, the agricultural population stubbornly against it." Before Chartism swallowed up the Anti-Poor Law agitation, some of these critics had to be left by the wayside. Oastler was one of the first to be left, Parson Bull of Bradford a second. There were to be many flirtations between Tories and Chartists in the future, but from the spring of 1838 onwards it was abundantly clear that Chartism would depend on its own leaders and not on alliances with people outside its ranks.

There was a final complication. Although the 1834 Act was detested by popular leaders in all parts of the country, its principles were supported by many Radical members of Parilament, including Joseph Hume, Daniel O'Connell and some of the closest friends of the London Working Men's Association. Some of the members of the LWMA themselves believed in "Malthusian principles." It was within a circle of men not basically unfriendly to the Act of 1834 that the Charter itself was being drafted. Bitterness between O'Connell and O'Connor had an ideological twist to it, and differences between the LWMA and other working-class groups in London included differences of approach as well as of background. Before the Charter was published, some of the main conflicts within Chartism were clear for the world to see. Julian Harney, for example, one of the most interesting and articulate London Jacobins, attacked the LWMA not only on the platform but in the correspondence columns of *The Times*. Almost all the later divisions in Chartism can be studied in microcosm in the London disputes of 1835, 1836 and 1837. Men like Harney were just as bitterly opposed to the New Poor Law as the handloom weavers in the north, and while missionaries of the LWMA were spreading their propaganda quietly and effectively in the provinces, links were being forged between the enemies of the LWMA in the East End of London and the leaders of discontent outside. The defeat of a considerable number of Radical members of Parliament at the general election of July 1837 redirected Radical energies back into public agitation, but the Radicals were unable to direct provincial discontents because of their equivocal or even hostile attitude towards the views of some Chartists of the future. Just as those Tories, like Earl Stanhope, who dreamed of a national federation of Anti-Poor Law societies, pledged to repeal of the Act of 1834, could not take the lead in the years of increasing discontent, so those Radicals who believed in a substantial measure of parliamentary reform were doomed to play a restricted and limited part in popular agitation. Their ideas were written into the Charter, but ideas were not the most important elements in the political equation.

The business depression was more significant than any other factor in setting the tone of national agitation. In the years of relative prosperity, good harvests and expanding trade between 1832 and 1836 most working-class energies had been absorbed in trade-unionism. The Grand National Consolidated Trades Union was only one example of a number of attempts to form large unions designed not only to raise wages but, in a phrase of Bronterre O'Brien, to bring about "an entire change in society—a change amounting to a complete subversion of the existing order of the world. The working classes aspire to be at the top instead of at the bottom of society—or rather that there should be no top or bottom at all." The architects of the new unions dreamed of a new kind of social organization where Parliament would be replaced by a "House of

Trades," and they put forward ambitious claims for the Grand Council of the GNCTU. "There are two Parliaments in London at present sitting," wrote J. E. Smith, the editor of the *Crisis* in 1834, "and we have no hesitation in saying that the Trades Parliament is by far the most important, and will in the course of a year or two be the more influential." Although Robert Owen explicitly repudiated universal suffrage, James Morrison, the editor of the *Pioneer,* related this objective to trade-union growth and talked of an "ascendant scale" by which universal suffrage would be realized. "With us universal suffrage will begin in our lodges, extend to the general union, embrace the management of trade, and finally swallow up the political power."

The reasons for the failure of trade-unionism lay not so much in the pricking of these giant bubbles—they fairly quickly pricked themselves—but in the resistance both of employers and local authorities to specific local trade-union claims. Before the prosperous years drew to a close, trade-unionism had been almost completely destroyed as a nation-wide force. Owen himself, who had never agreed with the views of many of the unionists and had failed to understand the nature of the agitation he had helped to inspire, retreated without regret into sectarianism, to a renewed emphasis on "the principles of the New Moral World in all their extent and purity." "I am termed a visionary," he had told Ricardo years before, "because my principles have originated in experiences too comprehensive for the limited locality in which people have hitherto been interested." The origins of Chartism as a national movement are to be discovered, as we have seen, in the "localities." Before another movement with large claims could be constructed, there first had to be a breaking down of utopian hopes as well as of vast organizations, for Chartism grew not only out of hunger and anger but out of disillusionment, disillusionment both with the Reform Bill of 1832, widely regarded as a "sham," and with the ambitious trade-unionism of the "good years." When Henry Hetherington, the close friend and collaborator of William Lovett, visited Leeds in 1834 after the collapse of local trade-union efforts he drew the moral that nothing less than universal suffrage would break the workers' chains. It was a moral which the *Poor Man's Guardian* preached on every available occasion, and it was a moral which the Chartists took up in 1838. By that time many grievances had accumulated in all parts of the

country, and the snowball metaphor which Morrison first applied to
trade-unionism was even more applicable to Chartism.

There were links between trade-unionism and Chartism as well
as differences of approach. Some local trade-union leaders, but by
no means all, were Chartists a few years later. When the Dorchester
laborers were sentenced to transportation, it was Lovett who was
secretary of the national committee of protest set up in 1834. The
committee included many of the men who later drew up the Charter,
and collected subscriptions from all the trades which contributed
most to the LWMA—tailors, shoemakers, joiners, cordwainers and
coachpainters. It summoned protest meetings in all parts of the
country—in factory districts, country towns and large cities as well
as the metropolis. Three years later when the "new Tolpuddle
martyrs," the leaders of the Glasgow cotton spinners, were sentenced in January 1838 to seven years' transportation there was a
further outburst of working-class indignation. On this occasion, however, some of the differences which were to dog Chartism were again
openly demonstrated. Daniel O'Connell was an outspoken critic of
the trade unions, as were some of the other Radical members of
Parliament, and when he successfully moved in the House of Commons for the setting up of a select committee to inquire into work-
ingmen's combinations, O'Connor, Harney and the *Northern Star*
launched a direct attack on the LWMA for supporting this maneuver.
The ensuing quarrel between O'Connor and the LWMA exceeded in
bitterness any that had arisen before, and in a sharp letter Lovett
not only denied the charges but accused O'Connor of seeking to
pose as "the great *I am* of politics." "You would have it believed,
to our prejudice," the letter concluded, "that we have been neglectful
of the working men, because we choose another path from yours.
But time will show, and circumstances soon determine, who are their
real friends; whether they are 'the leaders of the people' who make
furious appeals to their passions, threatening with fire and sword,
or those who seek to unite them upon principles of knowledge and
temperance, and the management of their own affairs."

Within a few months of the writing of this letter the Charter had
been published and the first steps were being taken to organize the
election of delegates to the "General Convention of the Industrious
Classes." It was clear from the start that there would be dramatic
differences. The local materials out of which nation-wide Chartism

was forged were many and various, and the founders of the movement were in disagreement about both tactics and social objectives.

George Rudé

THE CROWD IN THE FRENCH REVOLUTION OF 1848

George Rudé is an Englishman who taught for many years at the University of Sydney, and is currently a member of the Department of History of Sir George William University, Montreal. Rudé has written about other subjects, but most of his work has been about the "crowd," for he has studied it in its various manifestations—as a food riot, a city mob, a Luddite group, a political demonstration, a revolutionary crowd—in France and England in the eighteenth and nineteenth centuries. Twelve of his shorter studies plus four synthetic essays have been published as The Crowd in History (1964). Our selection is drawn from this book. It is typical of Rudé's method: it analyzes the economic, political and intellectual context, describes the actions of the crowd, assesses its success, and attempts to discover "the faces in the crowd" and their motives and beliefs. In this article, Rudé finds the 1848 crowd to be transitional, largely artisanal or preindustrial, with an admixture of new industrial workers. The crowd in the Paris Commune of 1870 was similar, except that the number of new workers had increased.

Two factors, perhaps more than any others, ensured that the crowds in the French revolution of 1848 would not be identical with those of 1789. One was the beginning (but only the beginning) of modern industry; the other the spread of socialist, or near-socialist, ideas among the industrial and working population. The factory system and mechanization had taken root in the textiles of the north and east, in mines, chemicals, silk, soap, sugar refineries, and parts of metallurgy: in 1847, 5,000 steam engines were in use where, seven years before, there had been only 2,000. The railways had also made their appearance in the 1840s: by 1850, 2,000 miles of track had been laid,

From George Rudé, "The French Revolution of 1848," in his *The Crowd in History* (New York, 1964), pp. 164–177. Reprinted by permission of John Wiley & Sons, Inc. Footnotes omitted.

and Paris had new rail repair workshops at St. Denis and the village of La Chapelle. Yet, outside these industries, the "revolution" had made little progress: three-quarters of France's population still worked on the land and her industrial workers continued, for the most part, to be employed in the workshops and cottages of sixty years before. The population of Paris had grown to a little over a million; but apart from her railways and engineering shops she was still a city of manufactories, homeworkers, and petty crafts; and the small workshop, far from disappearing, had increased its hold. There were still only five workers to every employer; and the main centers of the working population were still the old faubourgs and markets of 1789, though now extending north, south, and east into industrial suburbs that were villages half a century before. The age of the great industrial employer, like that of the factory worker, was yet to come. It was the banker, the merchant manufacturer, the speculator and owner of real estate, and not the industrialist, that ruled the roost and formed the backbone of what Marx termed "the Joint Stock Company for the exploitation of France's national wealth"[1] (and Tocqueville said much the same), and to whom Guizot gave his comforting cure for social ills: "Enrichissez-vous!"

Though social and industrial change was slow, ideas were breeding fast; and the 1830s saw a remarkable development in the political education of the French industrial population. In the revolution of 1830, workers had left their workshops to take up arms and overthrow the monarchy of Charles X; and as far as can be told from limited records there were many workers among those decorated for their part in these events and among those killed and buried beneath the "column of July."[2] Yet this was only a repetition, though on a larger scale, of what had happened in 1789 and 1792; and the workers were in no position, once the revolution had been made, to affect its course.

What was new in the 1830s, following the July experience, was that workers were beginning to associate in organized groups— not merely on a workshop basis under their masters—to take part in political affairs. The first workers' newspapers, the *Journal des Ouvriers,* the *Artisan,* and *Le Peuple,* appeared in September 1830;

[1] Marx was referring to the regime, known as the July or Orleanist Monarchy.—Ed.
[2] The Revolution of 1830 occurred in July, and is often called the July Revolution. —Ed.

and, the first of the two great insurrections of Lyons silk weavers broke out in November 1831, under the slogan *Vivre en travaillant ou mourir en combattant.* It had far deeper social aims than a mere rise in wages or the provision of work, and although a joint outbreak of small masters and journeymen, it is generally held to mark the birth of the modern labor movement. It came at a time of wretched housing, low wages, and depression and was followed, in Paris, by a series of riots and armed insurrections, aimed not primarily at merchants and manufacturers but at the government itself. Among those arrested in the most violent of them all—that of June 5–6, 1832, in the cloisters of St. Méry, where 70 troops and 80 rioters were killed—we find several craftsmen, and journeymen whose names reappear in later riots: and one—a journeyman baker—who was re-arrested shortly after for taking part in a *coalition ouvrière,* or wage movement. It may seem trivial, but the point is of great significance: here for the first time we find the same workers being engaged in successive political demonstrations, wage demands being put forward at a time of economic depression, and wage earners participating as readily in political as in economic movements.[3] This had not been seen in earlier revolutions and represents a landmark in the history of working-class action and ideas.

Soon after the second Lyons outbreak in April 1834, this phase of political rioting ended, but the fermentation of political ideas continued. In the same year, the word "socialism" was first used by Pierre Leroux, and the ideas of Babeuf (via his old disciple Buonarotti), Blanqui, Barbès, Blanc, Cabet, Proudhon and the Saint-Simonians began to circulate among the workers. Their remedies ranged from mild reformist measures to the class war and popular insurrection preached by Auguste Blanqui; they stressed the need for equality of distribution rather than the public ownership of the nation's wealth; but they all addressed their remedies to one specific class, the workers; and this in itself was new. Under the impact of these ideas secret societies and clubs sprang up, such as Blanqui's Societies of the Families and of the Seasons and the Society of the Rights of Man, themselves the forbears of the far larger and more influential clubs, sometimes attracting attendances of 5000 and more, that played so important a part in and after the Febru-

---

[3] The overlap between political and economic movements is stressed here; in Stearns's article it is deemphasized.—Ed.

ary Revolution. Alexis de Tocqueville sensed the new spirit that these clubs engendered. In a speech to the Chamber in January 1848, he warned, the "working classes . . . are gradually forming opinions and ideas which are destined not only to upset this or that law, ministry, or even form of government, but society itself."

How far Tocqueville was right or wrong in his prognostication the revolution that broke out in Paris four weeks later would reveal. The outbreak, as is common on such occasions, developed in successive stages, from a demand for mild reform into a popular revolution. It started with a campaign, supported by the liberal opposition, to hold banquets in favor of an extension of the suffrage. When Guizot banned the banquets, the opposition leaders withdrew; and the radical and republican journalists of *Le National* and *La Réforme* took them over and organized great popular demonstrations in support. At this point the bourgeois National Guard, instead of dispersing the crowds, sided with the reformers; and the King, bowing to public opinion, dismissed the Guizot Ministry. But the demonstrations, far from subsiding, grew in strength and drew their main support from the popular quarters in the east and center of the city. In the Boulevard des Capucines, several demonstrators (some accounts say 50, others 100) were killed and wounded in a bloody encounter with the troops. This gave a new purpose and direction to the riots: gunsmiths' shops were raided for arms; and on the morning of February 24, Paris was in open revolt.

A succession of opposition leaders now tried to form a government, but it was too late; and when the armed insurgents bore down on the Tuileries, the King abdicated and fled to England. An attempt was made to form a Regency for the child Comte de Paris; but crowds invaded the Chamber, brushed the old constitution-makers aside, and received with acclamation a new "provisional" government, drawn up from lists of names submitted by the radical journalists, including those of the radical leader, Ledru-Rollin, and the poet Lamartine. But the crowds, mindful of the "betrayal" of 1830, were determined to reap their own share of the common victory; and the government when publicly proclaimed at the Hôtel de Ville bore two added names: those of the socialist leader Louis Blanc and the metalworker Albert. Yet this was by no means all. During the next days, massive demonstrations at the Hôtel de Ville, backed by the socialists and clubs, wrung from the Provisional Government a number of concessions: the promise of "the right to work"; "national" workshops for the unemployed (a distortion of Blanc's demand for state-run "social" workshops, but a concession nonetheless); the right to organize in unions; the 10-hour day; the abolition of debtors' prisons; male adult suffrage; and the immediate proclamation of the Republic.

Thus the wage earners had not only, as in 1789 and 1830, helped to make a revolution; once the initial victory had been won, they had continued to leave their mark upon it. In earlier revolutions, they had taken their ideas and slogans from the bourgeoisie, even if occasionally adapted to their own use; this time, they were organized in their own political clubs and trade associations, marched under their own banners and leaders, and were deeply imbued with the new ideas of socialism. Nevertheless, the revolution, still less its fruits, was not entirely theirs. As on similar occasions in the past, they had left their workshops with their masters and, with them, jointly manned the barricades; radical journalists, students, *polytechniciens* and National Guards had also played their part; and on the lists of those decorated for their part in the February events the names of wage earners appear alongside those of shopkeepers, master craftsmen, and members of the liberal professions. Tocqueville, in fact, saw only one side of the picture (though admittedly to persons like himself the most alarming) when he wrote that the workers were the sole victors of the revolution and the bourgeoisie its principal victims; and that socialism had been its "essential characteristic." The workers had indeed won important concessions, but they were only temporary, and the government to all intents and purposes remained in bourgeois hands; a fact that would become the more apparent as the weeks went by. Moreover, if in Paris the wage earners had been able to give a new form and content to a popular revolution, in the provinces the older forms prevailed. In Alsace, Jewish homes and synagogues were wrecked (as in 1789), at Bourg a monastery, at Besançon the *mairie,* in Allier the customs, and in the Pyrénées and the Paris region the châteaux of the aristocracy. The state forests were ravaged in Ariège and Var; peasants rose in defense of ancient communal rights; and in an orgy of "Luddite" fury railways were torn up and bridges destroyed on the Paris-Rouen and Paris-Brussels lines and power looms and textile mills destroyed in Champagne, the Nord, and Normandy. Even in Paris, mechanical presses were wrecked by printing workers, so that the workers' paper, the *Atelier,* felt constrained to call on its readers to "respect the machines."

February 1848, then, despite its important innovations, only marks a half-way stage between the older type of popular movement and disturbance and the new. The Paris insurrection that in June ranged *ouvriers* and *bourgeois* on opposing sides of the barricades would carry the transition to a higher point. The June "days" had their remoter origins in the breakdown of the alliance between *bourgeois* democrats and workers that followed soon after their common victory in February. The sight of workers in their *blouses,* or peasant smocks, mounting guard over public buildings and flocking to air their grievances and dictate their terms at the Luxembourg Palace, where Louis Blanc had set up his "workers Parliament," had begun to alarm many who, though revolutionaries and republicans in February, shared Tocqueville's concern that "property" might now be threatened. Further apprehension had been roused by the great workers' rally organized by Blanqui on March 17. A month later, the clubs and Blanc's Luxembourg Commission combined to stage a vast workers' demonstration, whose objects were to postpone elections to the new Assembly (the provincials were rightly suspected of not sharing the Parisians' revolutionary spirit), and to press the government to create a "democratic Republic" based on the "abolition of the exploitation of man by man" and the "organization of labor by association." The nonsocialist members of the government took fright, and Ledru-Rollin, in alliance with Lamartine, called on the National Guard to counter-demonstrate. At the Hôtel de Ville, it was the delegates of the National Guard who were received with honors; the workers' deputation was cold-shouldered and greeted with shouts of "down with the Communists!" The breach between the government and socialists was now complete.

The national elections followed a fortnight later and were a triumph for Lamartine's republican moderates, who won over 500 seats; even the combined monarchists—Orléanists and Legitimists—won 300 seats; while the socialists and their allies returned less than 100 members. The result was hailed by *Le National,* Lamartine's paper; and its radical rival, *La Réforme,* frankly saw it as "the defeat of the democratic and social Republic." In an attempt to redress the balance, the club leaders decided on another "insurrection." On May

15, their unarmed followers, supported by 14,000 unemployed workers from the government's national workshops, invaded the Assembly,
ostensibly to present a petition in favor of war with Russia in defense
of Poland. In the confusion that followed, some of their spokesmen
declared the Assembly to be dissolved and read out, as in February,
a list of new members of a provisional government, including Ledru-
Rollin, the socialists, and leaders of the clubs. This may have been
the intention all along, though it seems unlikely, as the demonstrators
were unarmed and once the National Guard was brought onto the
scene were easily rounded up and dispersed. The Assembly and the
Executive Council, however, decided to treat the incident as a pro-
jected coup d'état and to teach the workers and socialists a lesson.
Il faut en finir! Blanqui, Raspail, Barbès, and Albert, and about 400
others, were arrested. Blanc's Luxembourg Commission was closed
down; and five weeks later the national workshops, whose 115,000
inmates were both a drain on the public purse and no longer im-
mune to socialist agitation, were ordered to be dissolved.

The Executive Council's decree ordering the closure of the workshops was issued under the signature of Marie, the Minister of Public
Works, on June 21. The workers were faced with the alternative of
enlisting for the army (if 18 to 25 years of age), of being sent to drain
the insalubrious marshes of Sologne, or of remaining in Paris without
work or pay. It was an act of considerable provocation and to some,
at least, it appeared that its consequences had been intended.
Though deeper resentments, fed by weeks of frustrated hopes and
disappointments, lay at the back of the civil war that followed, this
was the spark that touched it off. The most vigorous of the workers'
leaders were in prison; others, like Blanc, who had escaped arrest
in May, urged caution; so, for lack of better, it was a strange mystic
(a self-styled "prophet of misfortune" and "days of blood") and workshop foreman, Louis Pujol, who became their spokesman. On June
22, 1,200 to 1,500 workers, with banners flying, assembled at the
Panthéon and sent a deputation of fifty-six delegates to parley with
the government at the Luxembourg Palace. Marie, who received Pujol
and five others, treated them with scant courtesy and replied to
Pujol's threats with counter-threats. The same night a torchlight
meeting, addressed by Pujol, was held at the Bastille; and another,
early the next morning, took the familiar pledge "Liberty or Death!"
As the marchers returned along the boulevards, the cry went up "to

arms!" and the first barricade, made of overturned buses, mattresses, and paving stones, was erected near the Porte St. Denis on the Boulevard Bonne-Nouvelle.

The insurrection lasted three days and spread far beyond the ranks of the workshop workers. Its main centers were the old popular districts of earlier revolutions: the Faubourgs St. Martin, du Temple, and Poissonnière to the north; the Place de la Bastille and the Faubourg St. Antoine to the east; the Cité (though not the Hôtel de Ville) in the center; and the Place du Panthéon, the Faubourg St. Jacques, and Latin Quarter to the south. Beyond the old city limits of 1789, the centers extended into Montmartre in the north and Gentilly in the south. Thirty-eight barricades appeared in the Rue St. Jacques alone, 68 between the Hôtel de Ville and the Bastille, and 29 more along the great popular highway of the Rue du Faubourg St. Antoine. The insurgents had little trouble in finding arms: many were old soldiers, more were National Guards (including officers) from the eastern legions. They may have numbered as many as 100,000. This, as least, was the number of muskets later seized in the insurgent districts. And their aims? The immediate demand was twofold: to restore the national workshops and to dissolve the Assembly that had closed them down. As other workers joined the insurgents, other aims were added. Banners fluttering from the barricades bore such slogans as "Organization of labor by association," "Abolition of the exploitation of man by man," "Respect private property, death to looters," and "Bread and work, or Death"; and the few proclamations issued voiced the familiar demand for "the Democratic and Social Republic."

To deal with the rebels, the government could muster 30,000 troops of the line, 16,000 *gardes mobiles* (mainly recruited from young laborers and unemployed), 2,000 Republican Guards; and, theoretically, the National Guard. But only the Guards of the western districts could be relied on: the eastern battalions had joined the insurgents; and, of those in the center, only 4,000 out of 60,000 responded to the government's call. In the event, General Eugène Cavaignac, who was given the supreme command of the government's forces, pushed forward the *gardes mobiles* and the National Guards of the bourgeois districts, while holding the bulk of the regular troops in reserve. As the fighting developed, however, the railways brought powerful support in the form of volunteers from all parts of the country. "Among them [wrote Tocqueville] were many peasants, many shopkeepers, many landlords and nobles, all mingled together in the same ranks. . . . It was evident from that moment that we should end by gaining the day, for the insurgents received no reinforcements, whereas we had all France for reserves."

After the first shock and confusion, the outcome was, in fact, hardly ever in doubt. The insurgents had touched a deep chord of response among the Paris working population, but they had no leaders other than those thrown up by the occasion; many socialists refused to join in, others joined only after the fighting had started. Above all, as far as the rest of France was concerned, the Parisian workers were out on a limb. On the first day, a triple attack by government forces failed to dislodge the insurgents from any but minor points of resistance; but the next day they lost the northern Faubourgs of St. Denis, Poissonnière, and du Temple and, on the Left Bank, the Place du Panthéon and the Montagne Ste. Geneviève. On the twenty-fifth, the forces of order succeeded in mopping up the last centers of resistance in the north and south of the city; and the rebels aroused indignation by the shooting (in the second case, by a stray bullet) of General Bréa and the Archbishop of Paris, both of whom had come to offer mediation. Only the old revolutionary stronghold of the Faubourg St. Antoine (as in May 1795) still held out. On the morning of the twenty-sixth, a deputation offered to lay down arms in return for an amnesty; but Cavaignac insisted on an unconditional surrender and soon after the battle resumed was able to enforce it. The insurrection was over.

The Assembly and propertied classes had been thoroughly alarmed, and the repression was correspondingly severe. Many had been killed in the course of the fighting, or massacred by the Mobile Guard: the police return of 2,000 killed and wounded is probably an underestimate. Fifteen thousand persons were arrested; but, since many had been rounded up as suspects for the mere fact of wearing the worker's *blouse,* 6,374 were, after cross-examination, released without trial or sentence. Over 4,000 were sentenced to prison, fortresses, or transportation to Algeria; only the assassins of General Bréa were guillotined. A commission met to inquire into the remoter causes of the disturbance. Ledru-Rollin, though attacked in the Assembly for complicity in the affair, escaped prosecution; but Blanc, innocent as he was of even the remotest connection with the outbreak, had to seek refuge in England to avoid trial. The clubs and revolutionary journals were closed down. Rid of the socialists and the fear of further workers' demonstrations, the Assembly settled down to dismantle what remained of the "social" Republic and to erect one that corresponded better to the interests of the victors.

Who were the insurgents and what had the insurrection been about? Marx and Tocqueville, though belonging to opposing camps and differing as to details, were both firmly agreed that it had been a struggle of class against class and marked a turning point in France's history. "What distinguished it," wrote Tocqueville, "among all the events of this kind which have succeeded one another in France for sixty years, is that it did not aim at changing the form of government, but at altering the order of society. It was . . . a struggle of class against class, a sort of Servile War." To Marx it was, more precisely, a struggle of "proletariat" and "bourgeoisie"; and he added, in words almost identical with those of Tocqueville, that from now on revolution (and not only in France) meant "overthrow of bourgeois society, whereas, before February, it had meant overthrow of the form of state." To contemporaries, who had no squeamish feelings about terms like "class war," neither statement would have appeared extreme: it was generally accepted (and there would be no point in picking out evidence to prove it) that the June revolt was an armed protest of the Paris workers, if not against the capitalists, at least against the property owners or "the rich."

Is the point equally acceptable to us, or does it require revision? The conflict was certainly not one between factory workers and their employers: this would have been impossible in the circumstances of the time. Paris, as we have seen, was still a city of small workshops and crafts that had little changed, in this respect, since the first great revolution of 1789. If we examine the occupations of the 11,693 persons who were charged in the affair, we find a remarkable similarity to the trades of those who stormed the Bastille and captured the Tuileries sixty years before. We find among them no fewer than 554 stonemasons, 510 joiners, 416 shoemakers, 321 cabinet makers, 286 tailors, 285 locksmiths, 283 painters, 140 carpenters, 187 turners, 119 jewelers, and 191 wine merchants; and most of these occupations are among the dozen largest categories to which the prisoners belonged. It is even likely—though here the evidence is not precise enough to be conclusive—that among these prisoners, small masters, shopkeepers, and independent craftsmen outnumbered wage earners, possibly by as much as two to one. Rémi Gossez, a French historian who has studied the question far more deeply than any other, adds the point that, because of the government's predisposition to consider all *hommes en blouse* as potential rebels, the proportion of workers among those arrested and released was considerably higher than among the smaller number of those actually convicted. Moreover, he goes on to show that there was no clear-cut division between the two opposing forces: workers served in the National Guard alongside property owners, shopkeepers, clerks, and professional men; the Mobile Guard was largely composed of young workers, many of whom had fought on the barricades in February; and, of industrial employers, most remained neutral in the fighting in order to guard their factories and shops, while several fought with their employees in the insurgents' ranks. From this he concludes that, while the social conflict was genuine enough, it was one that ranged small producers, lodgers, and sub-tenants (and not only wage earners) against shopkeepers and merchants, and against landlords and "principal" tenants (often shopkeepers), rather than against factory owners, masters, and industrial employers.

Such points are worthy of attention, and they suggest that in some respects at least the June insurrection looks back to older forms of social protest by small consumers and producers. . . . Striking as certain of the similarities between the crowds in 1789 and June 1848 are, however, the differences are equally great. In the first place, in the earlier revolution, the initiative was generally taken by the workshop masters, who were more literate and more highly politically educated than their apprentices and journeymen, and the traditional crafts played the major role in popular insurrection. This time the case was somewhat different. The initial impetus, as we have seen, came from the workers in the national workshops: this in itself was something new, as when similar workshops were closed down in Paris in 1789 and again in 1791 it hardly caused a ripple in the struggle of the political parties. Yet, in June, it was only a minority of the workshop workers that took part: a fact due, no doubt, to the government's decision to continue paying wages even after the fighting had begun. The backbone of the insurrection came from other groups. Thus building workers account for the largest category of those arrested; and it was noted that each of the main centers of resistance was held by its own distinctive trade association: carters at La Villette, coal heavers and dockers along the St. Martin canal, bronze workers on the Boulevard du Temple, and joiners and cabinet makers in the Faubourg St. Antoine. But even more significant: industrial development, though slow and thinly spread, had brought in railways and the beginnings of mechanized industry; and among the arrested insurgents, alongside the joiners, cabinet makers and locksmiths of the older crafts and shops, we find the names of some 80 railwaymen and 257 *mécaniciens*. It was the workers in the railway workshops of La Chapelle, already a thriving industrial suburb to the north of the old city, who built some of the first barricades in the Faubourg Poisonnière; and we find railwaymen also joining port and riverside workers in manning the barricades on the Island of the Cité. These workers had since February been among the most highly organized and militant in the capital; Gossez describes them as forming "the vanguard of the insurrection."

The railways therefore played an ambivalent role. On the one hand, by bringing in trainloads of troops and provincial volunteers to swell the forces of order, they played a substantial part in crushing the insurrection; on the other hand, by creating a new type of industrial worker, they set a new stamp on the workers' movement that would have important consequences for the future. Marx (who, like Tocqueville, had not the advantage of studying police and military records) may have looked too far ahead when he wrote as though the Parisian proletariat was already fully formed; but he was certainly right to stress the new relations developing between the classes and their significance not only for France but for the rest of Europe. The Second Empire of Napoleon III saw another forward leap in industrial growth, in workers' organization, and in the relations between capital and labor; and soon such manifestations as *taxation populaire* and "Luddite" attacks on machinery, which still survived in 1848, would be almost as dead as the proverbial dodo.

Guenther Roth

GERMAN SOCIAL DEMOCRACY TO THE AVERAGE MEMBER

Like Arthur Mitzman, Guenther Roth is a sociologist (at the University of California, Davis) who has divided his attention between political labor history and the sociological theories of Max Weber. His incursion into the history of labor politics has produced a study of Social Democracy in Germany from 1871 to 1918 that does not confine itself to yet another examination of the party's intellectual debates and its bureaucracy. Instead he examines the broader role of The Social Democrats in Imperial Germany *(1963). This includes looking at Social Democracy as a subculture, a way of life significantly different from the dominant culture, yet connected to it. It also includes looking for what Marxism and the movement in general meant to its members. The first section of the excerpt suggests that the appeal of popular or vulgar Marxism lay in its expression of workers' desires, resentments and everyday experience; the second section shows that the movement itself satisfied workers' needs to belong and contribute to collective activities. The conclusion— that the workers themselves were nonrevolutionary—has much to recommend it, but it may be modified when recent studies of local parties are published.*

The deterministic component of Marxist ideology was apparently meaningful to both moderate and radical active party members, as well as to the passive followers of the movement. Relating Bebel's[1] popularity to his pronounced Marxist phraseology, Michels explained "the suggestive effect which Marxism in particular exerted on the masses" as a resultant of their strong desires and their passive tendencies. The worker "need only pay his party dues and at election time deliver his Social Democratic ballot. The rest will be taken care of by the 'development.'" Irrespective of whether there was a modal proletarian personality characterized by strong desires and passive tendencies—a theory which Michels took over from the psychologist and democratic politician Wilhelm Hellpach (1877–1955)—deterministic Marxism was indeed attractive to those who were relatively passive supporters. However, it could also motivate many party work-

From Guenther Roth, *The Social Democrats in Imperial Germany* (Totowa, N.J.: The Bedminster Press, 1963), pp. 199–211.

[1] August Bebel, a worker, helped pave the way for a united German Social Democratic Party. He was an SPD member of the Reichstag from 1874 to 1913, and Chairman of the Party Executive from 1892 to 1913.—Ed.

ers to great exertion in order to facilitate the "inevitable" development in accordance with Marx's dictum that it is possible "to shorten and lessen the birth-pangs of the new society."

For the workers to understand Marxism, it had to be vulgarized. The "Austro-Marxist" Otto Bauer, the leading theoretician of the Austrian party and its leader after the First World War, accepted this in 1907.

> *Deterministic Marxism is for the masses of workers not only a tremendous advance of knowledge, but also a motive power of their will . . . the reception of a new science by the masses is an historical process in the course of which the masses adapt the thoughts they want to understand to their capacity for comprehension at a given moment. From the history of the natural sciences and of philosophy many examples could be provided which show that the simplification and vulgarization of a new doctrine is nothing but a stage of its victorious advance, of its rise to general acceptance.*

The low level of comprehension had advantages as well as disadvantages. It handicapped the functionaries and the ordinary party members when greater knowledge would have made it easier for them to convince more workers or to defend more aptly the socialist position against bourgeois critique. Lack of knowledge combined with great enthusiasm for the new creed many times resulted in frustrations and antagonisms between the believers and their fellow workers. But the firmness of the naive belief in vulgar Marxism also afforded protection against the disillusioning realization of the theoretical difficulties of Marxism and of the complexity of political and social processes. When Joseph Buttinger, who cooperated and finally clashed with Otto Bauer in the Austrian underground movement of the 1930s, was appointed at the age of 24 to the very responsible position of a local party secretary, he delivered twelve carefully outlined lectures on the overambitious topic, "From the Primordial Nebula to the State of the Future"—a farewell address to the youth group he had led. Marxism, as he understood it, gave him more certainty than Catholic dogma had previously given him, and he set out unhesitatingly to explain to his audience problems which he himself did not adequately understand.

Of what did vulgar Marxism consist? In his memorial article on *Das Kapital,* Otto Bauer enumerates the various disjointed components of vulgar Marxism separately believed in by the masses, but considered to have scientific connection beyond their understanding:

> *The mode of production of material life determines the social, political and cultural process of life. It is not the consciousness of men which determines their existence, but their social existence which determines their consciousness.*
>
> *The history of all hitherto existing society is a history of class struggles.*
>
> *The value of a commodity is determined by the labor socially necessary for its production.*
>
> *The wealth of the propertied classes derives from the surplus value produced by the workers, from the unpaid labor of the working class.*
>
> *Capitalist society tends to increase more and more the misery of the workers.*
>
> *Small business will be destroyed; the control over the means of production falls into the hands of a continuously decreasing number big capitalists.*
>
> *Monopoly capitalism has become a fetter on the mode of production which arose under it and with it. The centralization of the means of production and the socialization of labor will reach a point where they will be incompatible with the external capitalist form. The final hour of capitalist private property is approaching. The expropriators will be expropriated.*

Bauer did not explain the appeal of the disjointed propositions to the workers. This was done later by de Man, who proposed an explanation of why and in what fashion key concepts of Marxian theory changed their original meaning in the process of adoption by large numbers of people. He contrasted the differential reactions of workers and of intellectuals to what they considered the iniquitous effects of industrialization. Their affects are similar, but the intellectuals attempt to arrive at valid theories while the masses transform these theories "by a regressive evolution . . . into symbols of affects." He argued that vulgar Marxism was successful because it corresponded to the everyday feelings and perceptions of the masses:

> *For instance, the concept of exploitation, which Marx based upon scientific argument, acquires a symbolical significance . . . in the minds of the masses. Millions of workers believe that Marx proved that the employers unjustly appropriate part of the value which they, the workers, create— namely surplus value. Among these millions, you will hardly find a few hundred who are capable of understanding Marx's arguments. The immense majority never attempt to get acquainted with them. Besides, the*

arguments have no bearing upon the symbolical use of the concepts "surplus value" and "exploitation." The symbolical use is entirely based upon the feeling the worker has, born out of experience, that he is being exploited. . . . the masses regard as fundamental that which Marx intentionally left in the shade, or tacitly assumed to be already proved, namely the moral stigma which attaches to the employing class for an unjust appropriation of surplus value. . . . Marxism is that which the labor movement, regarded as a totality of trends of emotion and will, has made of the theoretical system of Marx. Nothing else is alive in Marxism, for nothing else is able to create life, new social life.

However, de Man was aware that the beliefs of many workers, even if they seemed to coincide with their everyday experience, could often easily be disturbed when they had to face members of higher strata and were told, for example, that the top managers in industry were hard-working men and very important for economic progress. The class distance of workers from middle-class persons and especially the political distance of Social-Democratic workers from members of higher strata impeded or made impossible effective political communication. This had advantages for the labor movement and for vulgar Marxism because it decreased the competition from the ideas of the dominant system.

De Man's thesis that vulgar Marxism lent itself as an expression of desires, aspirations, resentments and everyday experiences of the workers may be accepted, but the ideological propositions and prescription alone would not have meant much if the labor movement had not offered the concrete experience of solidarity and of social recognition within a group of like-minded peers. Of course, Marxism provided a good rationale for the solidarity of the working class, but the collective experience was primary.

Solidarity and Collective Action

The attractions of solidarity and collective action can be illustrated in three different contexts: at the time of joining the movement, while doing lower-level party work, and during extreme political crises. A few examples, covering the whole period under investigation, may be mentioned. Anton Weiguny described in his memoirs the first attempts to organize journeymen tailors and garment workers (*Schneidergehilfen*) of small businesses in upper Austria in the 1870s.

The thrill of involvement in "serious" collective action for one's own economic group was so strong it enabled a radical break with past clique behavior and rivalry among different vocational groups of journeymen. The young workers suddenly became quite serious at the prospect of responsible group action. Weiguny's colleagues, each in his turn, sacrificed an hour's wage in order to read aloud during work hours, a practice previously observed by the tobacco workers.

When Buttinger was a 15-year-old boy, forced by his proletarian family's poverty to work on a farm, he experienced "the most sublime feeling" of his young life as 400 workers poured into his village to demonstrate against the mistreatment of a Social Democratic health insurance official: "Their appearance . . . awakened a sense of forces that would lift a man above the personal selfishness that, in the village, had shaped his outlook on life."

The "workers' poet" Karl Bröger (1886–1944) at first resisted demands to pay union dues, preferring to be forced off a job. Finally, he yielded to pressures. The conversion, with the experience of solidarity and the renunciation of individualism, came when he listened to the speech of a functionary who threatened a strike if a fired worker was not rehired:

He who yelled loudest and applauded most was [Bröger]. He was glowing with zeal and conviction. He nodded again and again and searched for the reflection of his own agitation in the faces of the others. Everywhere he found it. . . . He suddenly grasped the value and power of community and was anxious to support this newly found recognition. He began to talk about trade union problems, read what was worthwhile in this field, although he found it strange at first, and passionately accepted the socialist doctrine of salvation.

He had known that there were the rich and the poor and that there were more, infinitely more poor people. But he had been satisfied with this knowledge and derived from it the incentive to become rich himself. He had not been concerned with the goals of his own life sphere. Indeed, he had rejected his world, he had painfully tried again and again to transcend it spiritually. When he looked back, in the light of his socialist wisdom, on his youthful struggles, they appeared to him like the hopeless fighting of a soldier who, cut off from his troops, desperately carried on his own war. He believed the new order of life would come for all the poor, not just for one alone. It will come for everyone or it will not come at all. His difficult attempts during all those years were bound to end in defeat, for he had desired betterment only for himself; he had dreamed of millions

*of Marks to give him the good life in harmony with his tastes and capabili-
ties. He had no thoughts for other people or only those of a rich man
handing out alms. There is no right to personal happiness, there is only
the duty to further the general welfare.*

Sons of Social Democrats were likely to join the labor movement,
but not merely because of their fathers' example. A case in point is
William Bromme. He joined after the fall of the antisocialist legislation because of the appeal of "serious" collective pursuits.

At first Bromme did for the party only what his father demanded.
He carried socialist pamphlets and newspapers and shouted slogans
during an election campaign. For a while he sympathized, for reasons
not given, with the Advanced Liberals. He also spent much time with
a nonpolitical group of friends who had formed a regular "table
group" (*Stammtisch*) in 1889, unimaginatively called *Frohsinn,* as
many of the hundreds of German glee clubs were named. When he
first attended socialist meetings at the age of 16, he was much im-
pressed. Even the cheerfulness after the meetings appeared to him
different from the boistrousness of his glee club friends. At first, his
positive reaction may have been primarily due to the appeal of seri-
ousness and adulthood. But he gradually came to understand, as his
father had before him, that the combination of the workers was the
only means to improve their conditions. As isolated individuals they
could neither change their immediate nor their wider social environment. The labor movement offered a solution. As the father became
a victim of his political activity, the direct and indirect achievements
of the labor movement began to benefit his son. When the son was
dismissed for political reasons and indicted for political blackmail
in 1898, the organizations which the father had helped to build supported the son. Under the impact of the labor movement's growth,
the state accepted some responsibility for securing improved working
and living conditions. Bromme's mother died of tuberculosis; his
tubercular condition was treated under the provisions of the sickness
insurance. However, Bromme was incapable of further physical work
at the age of 33—the year that he finished his autobiography.

When Bromme writes that his political attitude and innermost conviction made him continue to work for the party, despite his ill health
and his wife's opposition, he bares only one part of the meaning of
the labor movement for him. His memoirs clearly reveal his personal
need for sociability and self-respect. Party work was the most mean-

ingful activity of his life. To give it up would have made him just a party member or voter, no longer belonging to the in-group of the local party organization.

This raises the problem of the meaning of the labor movement for the more active members, the lower-ranking functionaries in particular. A relevant example here is Adelheid Popp, who became one of the most prominent women of the Austrian labor movement. Her case shows that the material deprivations alone were not usually enough to make a worker turn to the labor movement. Adelheid Popp paints a picture of her youth exposing fully the physical and psychical mutilation inflicted on many men and women of the first lower-class generation recruited for large-scale industrialization. However, extreme suffering made her no more favorable to socialism than it made the thousands of other women at work in Viennese factories during the eighties. She believed the anti-Semitic propaganda and the characterization of Social Democrats as anarchists. But when she was without a job for several weeks her Catholic faith was shaken. Trials of Social Democrats aroused her compassion and interested her in the labor movement. After meeting her first Social Democrat in the eighties, she expected the revolution within a short time. Gradually her grasp of socialist ideas improved, and the party speakers and newspapers formulated for her those ideas she was unable to develop on her own:

> *I heard clearly and convincingly expressed that which I had instinctively felt but had never been able to think out. . . . The more consciously I became a socialist, the more free and strong I felt to meet all opponents.*

Reading pulp magazine fiction had kept her for several years in an imaginary world. Socialism, on the other hand, was concrete in a double sense: it was a theory explaining her material living conditions and promising a millennium, and a political movement to which she could belong. The labor movement provided her with meaningful work and an articulate class consciousness. Absorbed in everyday party work, she completely identified with the movement. This is what it meant to her to become a full-time functionary:

> *I was now endlessly happy. I had a sphere of work which satisfied all my longings but which I had considered quite unattainable for myself. It was to me the Promised Land.*

The intense identification with the labor movement and the great sense of personal satisfaction were shared by both moderate and radical functionaries. Both groups were equally interested in efficient organization, but the radicals, such as Buttinger, were also concerned with the Marxist indoctrination of the workers, particularly those who were already followers. The more radical functionaries could afford such concern because they did not carry the responsibilities, sustained by the top leaders, for the survival of the movement and for dealing with the government and the public; they could operate nearly exclusively within the classbound and isolated realm of the Social Democratic subculture. Many moderate functionaries, too, immersed themselves completely in this realm. Typical of them was Bromme. He was very useful as a member of a party which aimed primarily at increasing the number of its parliamentary seats and at expanding its organization. The considerable material sacrifices he made for the party were partly borne by his wife and children, who could not share the emotional gratifications which compensated him. He tried to avoid provocations, but was not deterred from party work by the ever present possibility of dismissal for political reasons, criminal prosecution on ad hoc pretexts or the danger to his health through overexertion. This is no mean record, but he was not the kind of man likely to impress the more radical functionaries. His absorption in administrative work, membership drives and electoral campaigning, to the more or less tacit exclusion of theoretical interests, placed him clearly in the ranks of the moderates, among whom the editor of his autobiography, Pastor Göhre, was prominent.

Just as the reasons for joining the labor movement and the activities to which an individual devoted himself shed light on the movement's meaning to each person, so the personal meaning became visible in those moments that threatened the very life of the movement. The events of 1933 proved that the beliefs of the Social Democratic and Communist functionaries and rank and file were not functioning to produce mass resistance against the destruction of the labor movement in Germany. Both movements collapsed when they were outlawed and confronted with totalitarian methods of suppression. But this is no argument against the assumption that the labor movement was the life center of masses of workers. Whenever suppression was not totalitarian, the importance of the labor movement for many members made them try to perpetuate its organizational life. There is a striking parallel between the events of 1878 in Germany and 1934 in Austria: Many members refused to give up what meant so much to them. The leaders, with few exceptions, lost much prestige and control when the confused members turned to them only to be disappointed. The descriptions by Auer, Vollmar and Mehring of the events after the outlawing of the German party in 1878 and Buttinger's account of the suppression of the Austrian party by the clerical fascists are very similar. The failure of the German leadership was cautiously acknowledged in 1889 by Ignaz Auer, who conceded that "the executive committee of the party lost touch with the majority in an exceedingly short time." Vollmar and Mehring were more outspoken. Vollmar agreed with those who accused the leaders of having abandoned the masses, and Mehring wrote in his history of the party that the masses and not the leaders saved the movement. The passage was later eliminated at the insistence of Auer and Bebel.

After 1878 and 1934 many members were soon rallied by energetic organizers willing to use more radical methods, who established an underground movement spreading outward from the big cities. Buttinger's description of many members' reactions to the suppression can probably be accepted for both situations. It clearly reveals the meaning of the movement for them:

> *To the faithful members and organizers of Social Democracy, the party ban amounted to brutal interference with their personal lives even if it failed to affect their economic existence. The possible loss of a few shillings a week meant nothing to those who now feared for the essence of their lives. The flags and symbols, the badges and pictures, the songs and legends of the "fight for freedom of the working class" had served many as substitutes for a lost religion and for . . . national patriotism. . . . For tens of thousands, party work was a self-evident duty, gladly performed. The very annoyance attached to all social activities seemed to tie them to it. Often—in choir singing, at giant rallies of the party, in admiring their leaders, and under the magic spell of the great incantations of their "world struggle for freedom"—they had lost their own sense of insignificance. A wonderful, self-surrendering mood would seize them and lend them a greater dignity, more self-assurance, more courage, and a stronger socialist faith. Those were the hours of their ultimate bliss—and of the knowledge that all beauty in their lives came from the better sentiments that had brought them to the socialist movement. There, by their unselfish, satisfying endeavors, they were tied up with greater ends—with the harmony the party preached between their daily political activities and a*

higher destination of man. To lose the party was nothing less to them than to lose home, fatherland, and religion.

The fact that the labor movement became "home, fatherland and religion" to hundreds of thousands points up their great alienation from the dominant system. But nearly all of the multitude of activities that made up the Social Democratic subculture were no direct threat to the dominant system.

The resurrection of the labor movement in 1878 in Germany and in 1934 in Austria was largely the result of the refusal of many members to give up inherently nonrevolutionary activities. In Austria, these exasperated and hampered the minority, which aimed at a revolutionary uprising. Thus, though the labor movement was the life center of many workers, this exalted meaning did not in itself constitute a revolutionary force. This was due in part to the moderating factors previously analyzed, but it was due as well to the fact that the Social Democratic subculture remained tied to the dominant culture in relevant respects, despite the depth of the class cleavage.

James Joll
ANARCHISM AND SYNDICALISM

James Joll, professor of international history at the London School of Economics, has published two books about anarchism, as well as two other books that touch upon the subject. In every one, he has been understanding, sympathetic and above all, fair, to a movement usually treated with condescension as a lost cause. Although he tends to deal with anarchism in a rather conventional way—he focuses on intellectuals and outstanding politicians—this is necessary to save anarchism from interpretations that emphasize its violent practice to the exclusion of its theory. This is not to say that he avoids describing acts of individual terrorism (propaganda by the deed) or conspiracies, for he does not. Nor does he deny the crucial role of the working-class movement known as revolutionary syndicalism in the broader anarchist movement. The excerpt from The Anarchist *(1964) reprinted here contains his ideas on revolutionary syndicalism and anarchism.*

Even before the Communist party in Russia had shown that a successful revolution was possible, and before Lenin's achievements had given new encouragement to Marxists as against anarchists, there had been many anarchists who were worried by the futility of individual terrorism and the sterility of academic discussions. Anarchism was, after all, a working-class movement. It was from among the workers that it had recruited many of its most devoted militants; it was in the daily recognition of the realities of the class struggle—at least in certain industries and countries—that its strength lay. The doubts about individual acts of propaganda by the deed and about the action of small conspiratorial groups, which men like Kropotkin and Elisée Reclus had often expressed, were reinforced by the increased pressure from the police and government after each act of terrorism. If anarchism were going to be more than an individual protest, it was going to have to find a new basis in the masses, and new means of action in an increasingly industrialized society. As Kropotkin put it: "If the development of the revolutionary spirit gains enormously from heroic individual acts, it is nonetheless true . . . that it is not by these heroic acts that revolutions are made. . . .

From James Joll, *The Anarchists* (Boston, 1964), pp. 194–205. Copyright © 1964 by James Joll. Reprinted by permission of Little, Brown and Company, and A. D. Peters and Company.

Revolution is above all a popular movement."[1] For anarchism to become a revolutionary popular movement in the face of the rival attraction of the growing political parties which the socialists were building, it needed to show its effectiveness as an organization capable of producing revolutionary social and economic change. As one anarchist paper put it at the time of the assassination of King Umberto I of Italy in 1900: "It is not the political head that we should be striking. It is the economic head, Property, that we must aim at."[2]

These ideas were, in a sense, a return to the classical anarchism of Proudhon and Bakunin.[3] They had never vanished from the anarchist movement, but, at least in the popular mind, they had tended to be overshadowed by the spectacular gestures of the individual terrorists and the resulting counter-measures which showed how seriously the police all over Europe took the anarchists. Proudhon had outlined a program by which the workers in their workshops would themselves take over the means of production without the need of political institutions; Bakunin, although largely concerned with the possibility of revolution among the backward peasantry of Russia or Italy, had also thought of the workshop or factory as a possible nucleus of social revolt. The only method of emancipation, he had written in 1869, is that of "solidarity in the struggle of the workers against the bosses. It is the organization and federation of *'caisses de résistance'*."[4] The anarchists of the Jura, concerned as they were with a day-to-day struggle to protect their interests, had responded readily to these ideas and they accepted the principle of direct action by the workers in pursuit of their own social and economic ends. As James Guillaume put it: "Instead of having recourse to the state, which only possesses such strength as the workers give it, the workers will settle their business direct with the bourgeoisie, will pose their own conditions and force them to accept them."[5]

The method by which this battle was to be fought was the strike, and already in 1874 one of the leaders of the Jura anarchists, Adhé-

---

[1] *La Révolte,* March 1891, quoted Maitron, op. cit., p. 240.
[2] *Les Temps Nouveaux,* August 1900, quoted ibid., p. 382.
[3] Proudhon and Bakunin were two of the intellectual "fathers" of anarchism: Proudhon, a Frenchman, lived from 1809 to 1865; Bakunin, an exiled Russian, from 1814 to 1876.—Ed.
[4] M. Bakunin, *Oeuvres,* vol. V, p. 182.
[5] *Bulletin de la Fédération Jurassienne,* 1 November 1774, quoted J. Maitron, op. cit., p. 261.

mar Schwitzguébel, put forward the idea of the general strike as the simplest and surest way of winning control of the means of production: "The idea of a general strike by the workers which would put an end to the miseries they suffer is beginning to be seriously discussed. . . . It would certainly be a revolutionary act capable of bringing about the liquidation of the existing social order and a reorganization in accordance with the socialist aspirations of the workers."[6] However, the watchmakers of the Jura were not numerous or powerful enough to create a large, effective organization, even though, in the difficult years after the Commune,[7] it was among them that the ideas of Bakunin were most vigorously and effectively kept alive.

It was in France that the new forms of industrial organization and tactics were devoloped; and they provided the anarchists with new possibilities of action—and also with new possibilities of disagreement. Whereas, in Germany and Britain, the new trade-union movements which developed in the 1880s were movements aiming at piecemeal improvement in the wages and conditions of employment of the industrial workers, and soon established very close relations with the growing socialist political parties, in France, from the time when trade-union activity was first permitted in 1884 after the repression following the Commune, the unions rapidly became committed to a doctrine of direct industrial action independent of any political parties. In the 1880s, it is true, Jules Guesde, the man most responsible for introducing Marxist ideas into French politics, tried to develop trade unions in close association with the Socialist party he had founded. However, the alliance did not last long, and at a congress of unions at Bordeaux in 1888 there was already a majority in favor of direct action by means of the general strike and against any political action. Finally, in 1894, the followers of Guesde walked out of a congress of syndicalists at Nantes. For some fifty years the French trade unions and Socialist party were to act independently of each other.

Meanwhile, it was on the basis of Proudhon's teaching that the new working-class organizations in France were being developed. These took two forms. In the first, the workers in individual factories,

---

[6] Quoted J. Maitron, op. cit., p. 261.
[7] The Paris Commune of 1871, which included some Bakuninists among its leaders, was brutally suppressed.—Ed.

and in some cases in individual industries, formed unions ("syndicats"). Secondly, from 1887 on, *Bourses du Travail* were formed alongside these syndicates. These were organized on a local basis, and workers in all trades belonged to them. The purpose of the *Bourses du Travail* was primarily to find jobs for workers, but they very quickly assumed functions beyond this and became centers for education and for the discussion of all the problems affecting the life of the working class. The movement spread rapidly and in 1892 the *Bourses du Travail,* already functioning in many parts of France, were linked into a national federation.

In 1895, Fernand Pelloutier was appointed the secretary-general of the *Fédération des Bourses du Travail,* at the age of twenty-eight, and it was he who made the movement into a powerful force and inspired it with a particular kind of anarchist idealism which not only influenced French working-class thought and action but also provided a pattern for other countries, notably Spain. Pelloutier came from a family of officials and professional men, originally Protestant, but converted to Catholicism in the early nineteenth century. He was sent to a Catholic school, but, although he was very intelligent, he failed to matriculate, and was, like so many of his generation, in trouble with the masters for writing an anti-clerical novel. His family lived in Brittany, and the young Pelloutier soon became the associate of a young lawyer in Saint-Nazaire, Aristide Briand, who was at the beginning of a long political career and, at this stage, a representative of the extreme left and much involved in the defense of anarchists and syndicalists in trouble with the authorities. Pelloutier's political activity in support of Briand soon got his father, a Post Office official, into difficulties and he was moved by the ministry to Meaux, and then, at the end of 1893, to Paris. Here Fernand continued his career as a spokesman and organizer of the working class, and within two years he was appointed secretary-general of the recently founded *Fédération des Bourses du Travail.* Here for seven years, in spite of ill health (he suffered from a painful and disfiguring tubercular affection of the face), he threw himself single-mindedly into the task of making the *Bourses* real centers for working-class education and a nucleus which would serve as a pattern for a future reorganization of society on the basis of workers' control of industry.

Although the numbers belonging to the *Bourses du Travail* were never very large, the ideas disseminated by them have never wholly disappeared from the French working-class movement. For Pelloutier the main task was, above all, the education of the workers and their preparation for their role in the new society. First of all, they had to be taught the rational basis for their instinctive revolt against the present situation: *"Ce qui manque à l'ouvrier, c'est la science de son malheur."*[8] The *Bourses du Travail* were accordingly to be "centers of study where the proletariat could reflect on their condition, unravel the elements of the economic problem so as to make themselves capable of the liberation to which they have the right."[9] Pelloutier and his followers believed that any trade-union movement must be truly revolutionary and aim at the total transformation of society, and that, at the same time, it must not fall into the errors of the society it intended to replace. "Must even the transitory state to which we have to submit necessarily and fatally be the collectivist jail?" he asked. "Can't it consist in a free organization limited exclusively by the needs of production and consumption, all political institutions having disappeared?" The workers' union was both a means of revolution and a model for the future. Thus the syndicalist movement "declared war on everything which constitutes, supports and fortifies social organization." Officers must be temporary; members must be free to leave. "What is a syndicate?" Pelloutier wrote. "An association you are free to enter or leave, without a president, having as its only officials a secretary and treasurer who are instantly dismissible."[10]

This was carrying Proudhon's ideas to their natural conclusion; and the anarchists were quick to see the possibilities of the new movement for the spread of their ideas. Already in 1892 the Paris police had seized a circular from the anarchist exiles in London instructing anarchists to use the syndicates as a method of action. The tactics were the same as those envisaged by Bakunin twenty-five years earlier (and to be put into effective practice by the *Federación Anarquista Ibérica* in Spain twenty-five years later). "It is very useful," the circular ran, "to take an active part in strikes as in all other working-class agitations, but always to refuse to play the star role. We must profit by every opportunity to make anarchist propaganda

[8] Maurice Pelloutier, *Fernand Pelloutier: sa vie, son oeuvre* (1867–1901) (Paris, 1911), p. 5.
[9] Ibid., p. 62.
[10] F. Pelloutier, *L'Anarchisme et les syndicats ouvriers*, in *Les Temps Nouveaux*, November 1895, quoted J. Maitron, p. 251.

and to warn the workers against the authoritarian socialists who will be the oppressors of tomorrow.[11] Pelloutier's ideas seemed to link this aim with a new and positive role for the anarchists in the working-class movement, and many anarchists joined the new syndicalist movement enthusiastically. Emile Pouget, for example, who edited *Le Père Peinard* and whose racy, popular journalistic polemics had made him a successful anarchist propagandist among the working class who wanted something more down to earth than the intellectual anarchism of a Jean Grave or a Kropotkin, became the editor of the main syndicalist weekly in 1900.

Pelloutier's main practical aim after he became secretary of the Federation was to amalgamate the revolutionary and educational activities of the *Bourses du Travail* with the action being carried on by the trade unions organized on a factory or industrial basis. The *Fédération des Syndicats et des groupes coopératifs* had been in existence since 1886; but in 1895 it split into two on the issue of whether to support political action by a political party. The majority adopted the view that Pouget had expressed a few years earlier when he wrote: "The aim of the syndicates is to make war on the bosses and not to bother with politics."[12] Once the supporters of Jules Guesde, who wanted a close association with the political socialist movement, had been defeated, the way was open for the syndicates to join with the *Bourses du Travail.* Nevertheless, the process was a slow one. The syndicates formed their own confederation (the *Confédération Général du Travail*— CGT) in 1895, but it was a comparatively weak and ineffective organization, and the almost total failure of a railway strike in 1898 marked how great the distance was between the hopes of effective and dramatic strike action and the actual capacities of the working class. Pelloutier was anxious that his comparatively strong and well-run Federation should not weaken itself by becoming submerged in a less efficient and less militant body; and, in fact, the unification of the syndicates and the *Bourses du Travail* did not take place in his lifetime.

Pelloutier died in 1901 aged only thirty-four. His tuberculosis had grown steadily worse and he had ruined his health still further by

[11] Quoted J. Maitron, *Le syndicalisme revolutionnaire: Paul Delesalle* (Paris, 1952), p. 24.
[12] Quoted J. Maitron, *Historie du mouvement anarchiste*, p. 252.

working not only as secretary-general of the *Fédération des Bourses du Travail* but also as editor of a review which was intended to provide the workers with serious articles and facts about the economic situation, and which Pelloutier and his brother produced almost unaided, even doing the actual printing themselves. Pelloutier's dedication, his mixture of practical gifts with moral enthusiasm, his devotion to the ideal of education and self-improvement among the workers, together with his early death, made him a legendary figure among his followers; and it was they who finally succeeded in uniting the *Bourses du Travail* with the CGT in 1902. Under the new charter, the CGT was composed both of syndicates and of *Bourses du Travail;* each section was autonomous, but each syndicate had to belong to a local bourse or an equivalent local organization. Thus the CGT was now based both on the federation of unions, and thus on the various industries, and on the federation of the *Bourses du Travail* and so on a system of regional and local decentralization. The spirit of Proudhon seemed to have triumphed.

However, although the syndicalist movement had now achieved a unity which in 1902 the French Socialist parties still lacked, and although they were committed to direct economic action and to opposition to all forms of political activity, they were, in fact, still very weak numerically. At the beginning of the twentieth century the industrial workers were in a minority in France. It is estimated that in 1906, 39 percent of the wage-earners in France were engaged in commerce and industry; and of these not more than 11 percent belonged to any sort of trade union, and only 4 percent to the CGT.[13] The membership fluctuated considerably according to economic conditions and between one industry and another. Thus any effective industrial action was bound to be limited in its results, unless it could succeed in paralyzing a key industry or service, such as the railways. Under these circumstances there was necessarily much disagreement about what the unions could achieve. Were they to be, as their anarchist members wished, militant organizations preparing the way by their example for the revolution and the new society? Or were they to be content with achieving what practical gains they could in limited sectors of industry? The discussion that divided the socialist political parties in these years, about whether reform or revolution

[13] Figures based on the 1906 census as given in Bernard Georges and Denise Tintant, *Léon Jouhaux: Cinquante ans de syndicalisme,* vol. I (Paris, 1962), p. 11.

was the first aim, was paralleled in the trade-union movement. The anarchists who saw in the unions a means of making the revolution were quite clear what they were trying to do. One of them, Paul Delesalle, who was one of the assistant secretaries of the CGT for several years, wrote that their role was to "demonstrate the foolishness of partial reforms and develop the revolutionary spirit among the union members."[14]

It was just because the syndicalist movement was weak that the idea of direct revolutionary action seemed attractive. If short-term gains were as hard to win as final victory, there was no reason why the latter should not be an immediate aim. Just as many German social democrats thought that the logic of history would bring them victory without their having to do very much about it, so many French syndicalists believed that somehow the capitalist order would fall at a single blow. The more serious militant syndicalists were constantly reproving this heresy. "If you only had to blow on the old society to overthrow it," Emile Pouget wrote on May Day 1904, "it would really be too easy. If we deceive ourselves about the size of the effort required, we are preparing for cruel disillusion. . . . The social revolution will not be accomplished without the necessity of a formidable effort."[15] Nevertheless, no one disputed the possibility of imminent revolution provided the will to it was there.

In 1906 the CGT formally accepted the views of militants like Pouget and recognized that it was a revolutionary organization which aimed at the seizure of economic power by means of direct action culminating in a general strike. Paul Delesalle described the plan of campaign as follows:

1. *A general strike by individual unions, which we can compare to maneuvers of garrisons.*
2. *Cessation of work everywhere on a given day, which we can compare to general maneuvers ("grandes manoeuvres").*
3. *A general and complete stoppage which places the proletariat in a state of open war with capitalist society.*
4. *General strike—revolution.*[16]

---

[14] Quoted J. Maitron, *Delesalle*, p. 81.
[15] Quoted E. Dolléans, *Histoire du mouvement ouvrier,* vol. II (2nd ed.; Paris, 1946), p. 117.
[16] J. Maitron, *Delesalle,* p. 111.

The problem which confronted the CGT was how to combine a state of war against capitalist society with the pursuit of immediate and limited gains for the workers. The months before the Amiens congress had been filled with industrial unrest; the campaign for the eight-hour day was in full swing and there had been extensive strikes in support of it, especially among the miners, who were the largest of the unions belonging to the CGT. The government had been sufficiently alarmed by the threat of demonstrations on May Day 1906 to order the arrest of the federal secretary and the treasurer of the CGT, and it was in this atmosphere of militancy that the CGT congress assembled later in the year. The congress reaffirmed the divorce between the syndicates and the socialist parties and laid down that, although members of the CGT were entirely free outside the unions to adopt the form of struggle which corresponded to their political or philosophical views, they were not to introduce these views in the unions; and the unions themselves should not "concern themselves with parties or sects, which are free outside and apart from the unions to work for social transformation as they think fit." What linked the members of the unions was a consciousness of the need to struggle for the abolition of the wage system and a "recognition of the class struggle, which, on an economic foundation, puts the workers in revolt against every form of exploitation, material and moral, that is operated by the capitalist class against the working class." At the same time, the Charter of Amiens tried to reconcile this with the need for day-to-day action in the following terms:

> *In respect of everyday demands, syndicalism pursues the coordination of the workers' efforts, the increase of the workers' welfare through the achievement of immediate improvements, such as the shortening of the hours of labor, the raising of wages, etc. This, however, is only one aspect of its work: it is preparing the way for the entire emancipation that can be realized only by the expropriation of the capitalist class. It commends the general strike as a means to this end and holds that the trade union, which is at present a resistance group, will be in the future the group responsible for production and distribution, the foundation of the social organization.*[17]

[17] The translation of these passages from the *Charte d'Amiens* is that given in G. D. H. Cole, *The Second International* (vol. III of *A History of Socialist Thought* [London, 1956], Part I, p. 371).

It is obvious how much this program owed to anarchist ideas, from Proudhon to Kropotkin and Pelloutier, but for some anarchists the assertion that the syndicates had a "double task of day-to-day activity and of the future" went too far in its implicit acceptance of existing society. There was, indeed, a formal public debate on these questions at an international congress, summoned by the Dutch and Belgian anarchists at Amsterdam in 1907. Many representatives of the young revolutionary syndicalists from France attended, together with many of the most respected international anarchist figures— Emma Goldman, the Dutchmen Cornelissen and Nieuwenhuis, Rudolph Rocker, and Malatesta—"perhaps," as one of the French anarchists put it, "the last representative of the old insurrectional anarchism."[18] The usual eccentrics were also present to make the proceedings more difficult; one of them objected on principle to any votes being taken, because this infringed the liberty of the minority, while another extreme individualist proclaimed that his motto was *"Moi, moi, moi . . . et les autres ensuite."* However, there was a serious discussion of the whole question of trade-union action which, according to reports from the various countries represented, was everywhere dividing the anarchist movement. For the young French syndicalists, Amédée Dunois and Pierre Monatte, the trade-union movement provided a means of bringing anarchism back to a direct contact with the workers. As Dunois put it: "By involving ourselves more actively in the working-class movement, we have crossed the gap which separates the pure idea . . . from the living reality. We are less and less interested in the former abstractions and more and more in the practical movement in action," and he went on to echo Pelloutier and say: "The workers' trade union is not simply an organization of struggle, it is the living germ of future society, and future society will be what we have made of the trade union."[19] Pierre Monatte, a twenty-six-year-old blacksmith's son from the Auvergne, made the connection between anarchism and the new syndicalism even more explicit. "Syndicalism," he said, "has recalled anarchism to the awareness of its working-class origins; on the other hand, the anarchists have contributed not a little towards putting the working-class movement on to the path of revolution and to popularizing the

---

[18] Amédée Dunois in *Congrès anarchiste tenu à Amsterdam 24–31 août 1907. Compte rendu analytique . . .* (Paris, 1908), p. 14.
[19] *Compte rendu,* pp. 36–38.

idea of direct action."[20] And for him, too, syndicalism was a moral as well as a social force: "Syndicalism does not waste time promising the workers a paradise on earth, it calls on them to conquer it and assures them that their action will never be wholly in vain. It is a school of the will, of energy and of fruitful thought. It opens to anarchism, which for too long has been turned in on itself, new perspectives and experiences."[21]

The idea of linking the future of anarchism to the trade unions was not, however, accepted by many anarchists. Emma Goldman, for example, was afraid that it might swamp the individual in a mass movement: "I will only accept anarchist organization on one condition: it is that it should be based on absolute respect for *all* individual initiatives and should not hamper their free play and development. The essential principle of anarchism is individual autonomy.[22] Malatesta, too, although he had always accepted some degree of organization and had, like Proudhon, thought that it was the autonomy of small social groups rather than of individuals that was important, was nevertheless worried that the new movement involved the risk of dividing the working class, since the interests of all workers were not necessarily the same, and that it might create a bureaucracy of just the type which the anarchists were working to abolish: "The official is to the working-class movement a danger only comparable to that provided by the parliamentarian; both lead to corruption and from corruption to death is but a short step." Above all, anarchism must not be limited to one particular class, even if it is the working class who most need revolution because they are the most oppressed. "The anarchist revolution we want," he said, "far exceeds the interest of one class; it has as its aim the complete liberation of humanity which is totally enslaved from three points of view—economically, politically and morally."[23]

Malatesta not only attacked some of the basic conceptions of the syndicalists; he also attacked their tactical methods. Revolution was revolution and could not be disguised as anything else. The bourgeoisie and the state would not give way without a fight, and once fighting started it was an insurrection—and this was not the same as

20 Ibid., p. 62.
21 Ibid., p. 70.
22 Ibid., p. 46.
23 Ibid., p. 85.

the general strike. "The general strike," he said, "is pure utopia. Either the worker, dying of hunger after three days on strike, will return to the factory hanging his head, and we shall score one more defeat. Or else he will try to gain possession of the fruits of production by open force. Who will he find facing him to stop him? Soldiers, policemen, perhaps the bourgeois themselves, and then the question will have to be resolved by bullets and bombs. It will be insurrection, and victory will go to the strongest."[24] The compromise resolution with which the discussion ended did not resolve the dilemma; but, as far as effective action by the anarchist movement was concerned, it was Monatte rather than Malatesta who was right. The ideas of anarcho-syndicalism and of direct industrial action were to give the anarchist movement a new lease of life; in France, at least until 1914, and still more in Spain, anarchism in association with trade unionism was to show itself, for the only time in the history of the anarchist movement, an effective and formidable force in practical politics.

[24] Ibid., p. 83.

W. Campbell-Balfour
THE LABOUR PARTY IN THE DEPRESSION

W. Campbell-Balfour of Cardiff, Wales, was one of more than two dozen members of the Commission Internationale d'Histoire des Mouvements Sociaux et des Structures Sociales who set out to study the impact of the Great Depression of 1929 to 1939 on the labor movement. Mr. Campbell-Balfour contributed two brief but penetrating articles on the impact on British labor; other members submitted articles on the effect on labor in most countries of Western Europe, Russia, the United States, and countries of Latin America and Asia. These articles were read and analyzed by three French scholars who compared them and drew some general conclusions. All the articles plus the comparative essay were published by the International Institute for Social History in Mouvements ouvriers et dépression économique. *A book of this type on such an important topic is so full of good work that it is hard to choose one example. Campbell-Balfour's essay was chosen because it dealt concisely with a whole complex of developments. In particular, it picks up on some of those noted by Hobsbawm.*

The important period of the 1930s in Britain should be set against the background of events in the preceding decade. There was an atmosphere of optimism in the ranks of British labor; the socialists felt sure of growing support as reaction from wartime events spread and their plans for a different form of society were more widely supported; the trade unions were in a boom situation with a shortage of labor and their membership grew rapidly to a peak of 8,348,000 in 1920, nearly twice that of four years previously. The period 1918–1926, culminating in the General Strike of 1926, showed the unions in a militant mood and more working days were lost per worker than at any time in the quarter centuries before and after the period. As Dr. Forchheimer indicates, the frequency or number of strikes "follow fairly distinctly the cyclical pattern." The curve of strike frequency rose from 1918 to a peak in 1920 then declined with the fall in prosperity.

There was a strong political element in the General Strike of 1926 which took place after this period of falling employment, falling prices and incipient stagnation in basic British industries, especially

From W. Campbell-Balfour, "British Labour from the Great Depression to the Second World War," in *Mouvements ouvriers et dépression économique* (Assen, The Netherlands, 1966), pp. 234–243. Reprinted by permission of the International Institute for Social History, Amsterdam. Footnotes omitted.

coal. The government subsidy given the coal industry to help maintain wages in 1925, was withdrawn the following year and precipitated the greatest strike in British industry which, in nine days, "involved 1.58 million workers and accounted for the loss of 15 million working days." The General Council of the TUC,[1] unprepared for a large-scale strike which was largely forced on them by the Conservative Government, were dismayed at the widespread response and showed less spirit than the celebrated Duke of Plaza-Toro who, though he "led his regiment from behind" did give them some support.

The collapse of the General Strike on the terms laid down by the government and employers meant the end of syndicalism as a theory. Another variant of this philosophy that industries should be controlled by the workers employed in them was Guild Socialism, which did at least provide for Parliamentary consultation and might be called a "pluralist" doctrine: this, too, suffered a serious setback with the failure of the Builders' Guild in the early 1920s. By the end of the decade, the trade unions had a rapidly diminishing membership (in 1929 it was nearly half that of 1920), a marked loss of idealism and faith in trade union action and philosophy, and less militancy.

These changes were partly due to the failure of the British economy to capture prewar markets and the overvaluation of the pound plus the rigidities of the Gold Standard, to which Britain returned in 1925 and abandoned in 1931; and partly to the retrogressive legislation passed by the Conservative Government in the year following the General Strike. Of this the General Council of the TUC reported, "Practically the whole trend of legislation for the past hundred years has been reversed by the present Government, who, through the Trade Disputes and Trade Union Bill, have tried seriously to impair the industrial and political power of the movement." This statement does not seem excessive, nor the conclusion that the Act left Trade Union law "ambiguous and confused."

Politically, the Labour Party of the 1920s had disappointed its supporters. Both the Labour Governments of 1924 and of 1929–1931 were minority governments, where Labour had to rely on the support of the Liberal Party with its traditional free trade policy and strong belief in a competitive economy, so that the two parties ran uneasily in double harness. They had also the misfortune to meet the full force

---

[1] Trade Union Congress. See the article by Hobsbawm, above.—Ed.

of the Great Depression. A different, though important factor, was that Ramsay MacDonald, Labour Prime Minister in both governments, whose popularity was so great in the twenties that it verged on idolatry, rapidly acquired [a] taste for the aristocracy and by 1931 openly preferred the peers to the proletariat. His defection to the Conservative Party in 1931 (although he retained the label of "National Labour") along with the Chancellor of the Exchequer, Phillip Snowden, caused confusion and bitterness. The Labour Party's parliamentary representation fell from 289 M.P.'s in 1929 to 52 in 1931, a defeat of staggering proportions. Though the Labour Party was reduced to shadow size in Parliament, only a handful followed MacDonald. The Labour vote remained surprisingly high, only the anomalies of the British voting system keeping them from increasing their number of M.P.'s. After 1931 the Labour Party began to piece together a program and a policy.

The trade unions had already begun to feel their way to a middle course between "bread and butter" unionism and the barricades. The TUC General Council suggested to the unions in 1928 that they had three choices:

> The first was to say, frankly, that the unions will do everything possible to bring the industrial machine to a standstill . . . in the hope of creating a revolutionary situation on the assumption that this might be turned to the advantage of the workers and to the abolition of capitalism. That policy the Trade Union Movement has decisively rejected. . . .
> The second course was one of standing aside and telling employers to get on with their own job, while the unions would pursue the policy of fighting, sectionally, for improvements.

This, too, was rejected by the TUC in favor of the third course, that the unions are concerned not only with the prosperity of industry, but also "the way industry is carried on. . . ."

By 1931, the early over-optimistic socialist dream had almost vanished. The internationalist belief that workers the world over who had a common cause, had disintegrated under the impact of Russian communism. The TUC took up an anti-Communist posture in the early 1920s which was made easier by the abuse to which they were subjected. Repeated applications by the British C.P. for affiliation to the Labour Party were rejected, while local Trades Councils who did not expel Communists were refused affiliation to the TUC. But the struggle was to continue throughout the thirties as the Communists took over the leadership of the unemployed workers' movements—under a variety of names ranging from the Minority Movement to the National Unemployed Workers Movement.

The unions turned their attention to holding their dwindling membership, adopting a cautious policy on strikes and disputes, while putting pressure on Parliament to combat unemployment. This had occupied much of their attention in 1930 when a strongly worded resolution was passed which declared that there might have been a revolution had it not been for the Unemployment Insurance Fund. The problem was approached characteristically as one of overproduction under capitalism, "where machinery and speeding-up of labor has increased the output per man, with the result that less men are required to produce the amount of goods which can find an effective market."

While no coherent economic policy had been worked out by the unions, there was an instinctive grasp of some of the remedies required, coupled however, with nostrums which would make the patient sick. Among effective suggestions was the statement that while a reduction in wages in one individual country might increase opportunities for export trade, it would reduce purchasing power on the home market. Further, a reduction of wages in all countries would leave foreign trade ratios unchanged while reducing mass purchasing power and aggravating the crisis. The TUC demanded an increase in expenditure on public works, to stimulate investment and income "in contradiction to the capitalist view, which demands a reduction of state expenditure in times of economic crisis."

In addition, the unions wanted an increase in unemployment benefits and a decrease in trade barriers and tariffs. As the economists were, as usual, neatly lined up for and against such policies, there was no large-scale support for the unions' views. The unions also coupled this expansionist policy with other suggestions for shortening the work week, raising the school leaving age, opposing industrial nationalization and the "speed-up" and extending paid holidays.

In the absence of government action on fiscal and monetary policy the unions tended to pursue a restrictive attitude to production, with craft unions closely regulating the entry of apprentices and objecting for several years to the encouragement of handicrafts in unemployed workers' centers. Elsewhere, workers fought the Bedaux system at several places and policies of "workspreading" were adopted—

though Pugh regrets in his book *Men of Steel* that the steelworkers would not "play the game" by their workmates and would take as much work as they could get.

By 1933, trade union membership had fallen to 4,392,000, its lowest figure since 1915. The number of working days lost through disputes in the thirties was also lowest in 1933 with only 959,000 days lost due to 134,000 workers (also a record low in this period) on strike. Wages were given as the reason for 42.1 percent of the disputes, with "employment of particular person" (which usually meant a nonunionist) coming second with 29.6 percent. By contrast with the American scene at this time, disputes over trade union recognition were as low as 4.7 percent. Indeed, from 1924 to 1937 this latter figure never rose to 10 percent while it remained close to 1 percent from 1930–1933. Nineteen thirty-one was a fair year for results of trade union strike action, with the unions winning 36.4 percent of disputes and 48 percent ending in a compromise, whereas in 1930, the employers scored their highest figure, winning in 77.8 percent of disputes. A high proportion, close on 50 percent, ended in compromise from 1931 to 1933, then this fell gradually to a low of 22 percent in 1939, indicating a struggle for more clear-cut decisions on both sides. This coincided with a rise in disputes, in working days lost and in trade union membership, which was 6,244,000 by 1939. Disputes settled through conciliation and arbitration fell from an average of 50 percent in the years 1929–1932 (1929 had an abnormal figure of 80 percent to just over 7 percent for the years 1933–1939.

In general, the number of working days lost through disputes was much lower in the thirties than in the twenties, especially from 1932 onwards. This period saw numbers of scattered strikes by small groups of workers ("quickies" as they are called in the United States). One reason for this decline in militancy, apart from the collapse of the Labour Government, the large-scale unemployment and the emotional and legal aftermath of the big strikes of the twenties, was the gradual extension of collective bargaining, already well established, into the less organized trades. This trend was supported by developments of Trade Boards practice and minimum-wage legislation. Trade Boards operate in the underorganized and low-paid industries so that they acted as a floor to wage movements in the later thirties. In this period the Conservative Government passed the Cotton Manufacturing Industry Act of 1934, the Agricultural Wages Act of 1937, and the

Road Haulage Wages Act in the following year. Under the Acts, associations of employers and employees or trade union representatives voted on wage rates and conditions of work and these were given statutory backing. Another variant of this was the extension of the Fair Wages clause of 1909, which says that contractors under government subsidy, protection or contract, must pay a wage equivalent to that of good employers in the trade in the district. Some of the industries falling under the clause were Housing, the Bacon industry, Films, Railways, Airways, and Sugar. Some eight million workers came under voluntary collective bargaining by the late thirties, three million under quasi-voluntary agreements and some two and three quarter million under statutory wage-fixing. Altogether, about 75 percent of agricultural and industrial workers were in some organization for wage determination.

One result of the Depression was that the unions strengthened their ties with the Labour Party and worked towards a common policy. This led, among other things, to the strange and transitory alliance of Ernest Bevin and G. D. H. Cole, the most powerful trade unionist and the leading socialist intellectual. This combination of the Pen and the Sword ended when the socialist propaganda group of Cole and Bevin merged with others of more apocalyptic and radical beliefs. One of the merging groups, however, was the New Fabian Research Bureau which played an important part in producing a series of pamphlets examining, in a serious and technical manner, proposals for the public regulation of banking, coal and public utilities, steel and transport, health services and insurance. They also passed on simplified versions of Keynesian employment theory in the late thirties.

An example of the close affinity of view between the Labour Party and the TUC emerges from the 1932 to 1935 trade union conferences. In 1932 the TUC, after consultation with the Labour Party, issued a statement supporting their policy of "no direct worker representation" on the boards of public industries. This was challenged first by Ernest Bevin and next by Charles Dukes of the General and Municipal Workers' Union, the next largest union to Bevin's, after Bevin accepted a compromise. Dukes' motion was twice narrowly defeated and was brought up again and accepted at a subsequent Labour Party Conference in Hastings. Dukes then reintroduced his motion and Walter Citrine, the General Secretary, modified his view from "whatever was decided at Congress would have to be carried out by the Labour Party" to a position of compromise when Dukes' motion was accepted at the Labour Party Conference then reintroduced at the TUC and Citrine agreed there must be "some attempt to create a unified policy. . . . We are ready to consult with the Labour Party. . . ."

Citrine was, however, correct in his view that the TUC could dominate Labour Party policy. The Constitution of the Labour Party stated that the Executive should consist of 23 members drawn from (a) the 13 representatives of affiliated organizations; (b) four representatives of women's organizations; (c) five from local Labour Parties; (d) the Treasurer. The voting to include the whole Conference. As "affiliated organizations" meant chiefly the unions, we can agree with MacKenzie that "it placed in the hands of the trade unions the power to determine the composition of the entire Executive." Almost alone amongst continental socialist parties, British Labour's political wing is the creature of the unions. From this it can be argued that Congress decisions will be binding on the Labour Party and are rarely reversed as the trade union vote in the Labour Party Conference varies from four-fifths to five-sixths of the total vote. There was a slight alteration to the Constitution in 1937, which strengthened the left-wing group by raising the local Labour Party representation in the Executive from five to seven and allowing these seven seats to be voted for only by the local parties. The local Labour Parties usually vote more radically than the Unions.

There was cooperation between the two wings of labor in the spate of pamphlets on social reform and planning poured out in the 1930s, most of which foreshadowed the 1945–1950 Labour Government program. A number of the Labour Party pamphlets are issued jointly with the TUC and early in 1933 there appears the first of many, "Hitlerism," on the menace of fascism to the unions and political democracy.

It should not be assumed that the two groups ran peacefully together in a three-legged race towards a benevolent and reformist socialist utopia. There was spirited opposition to "reformism" from the Communists and the ILP (Independent Labour Party) and some recalcitrant intellectuals waging guerilla warfare inside the Labour Party. The TUC, we have noted, had clashes with the unemployed workers' movements and refused to recognize them while they remained under Communist control. In spite of this ban, the militant activities of the Communists and their radical supporters brought out large demonstrations in the later thirties where many local labor parties and trade unions joined in. The Hunger Marches brought much public sympathy from the universities, and, almost to a man, writers and intellectuals were on the left. An occasional thorn in the TUC flesh was the Left Book Club, founded in 1936 by Gollancz, which combined the unusual features of political propaganda and publishers' profits. Left Book Discussion Groups were started all over Britain and more than 400 were claimed to be in existence at one time. The Left Book Club policy, under Strachey, Laski and Cole, gravitated towards a United Front policy with Communists and all those pledged to opposing fascism and Hitler. Though there were lengthy debates, both the TUC and the Labour Party rejected such an alliance. This was due somewhat to the trade union view that unity meant loyalty to the existing organization and the many "party within a party" groups that were formed were seen as "splinter" or possible breakaway forces. This view was characteristic of Ernest Bevin. When he later became Foreign Secretary he insisted, from his union experience, that his word must be loyally backed by the Parliamentary Labour Party. When there was dissension over Palestine, he accused his critics of "the stab in the back." They retorted by saying that he treated Moscow as a breakaway branch of the Transport and General Workers' Union.

Bevin and Citrine were the dominant trade union figures of the thirties: Citrine by his cool, logical analysis and his unremitting and successful opposition to Communist and near-Communist infiltration; Bevin by his crude though powerful debating manner and, not least, his control of the largest single block of votes at TUC and Labour Party Conferences. Beatrice Webb refers in her Diaries, where she labels trade union leaders as remorselessly, though not as skillfully, as a butterfly hunter, to the "silent opposition always glowering at them"—Bevin, Citrine and the trade unions. Bevin's power was shown at the 1935 Labour Conference where, after Lansbury, the Labour Party leader, had brought the hall to its feet by a moving pacifist appeal, he went to the rostrum and delivered a brutal and crushing attack which led to Lansbury's resignation and the later choice of Attlee as leader.

Nor was there complete unity in the ranks of the unions in their day-to-day work. There were hard struggles between unions over the whole period, indeed, in both the twenties and thirties, over demarcation disputes and recruitment policies. A resolution had been adopted in 1924 which attempted to regulate "poaching" of one union's members by another, but successive yearly reports contain lists of interunion disputes. A Disputes Committee was set up and passed judgment on cases laid before it. An example of the procedure will be found in the case of the Building Trade Unions versus the National Union of Public Employees. The decision begins:

> It shall not be the general policy of the National Union of Public Employees to enroll craftsmen in the building trades in competition with the craft unions.

We need hardly add that decisions are often given in favor of the larger or more powerful union, but the Disputes Committee served to show the growing stature of the TUC in the twenties and thirties. By 1939, after some twenty years of sporadic argument, the Bridlington Agreement provided a set of rules to regulate interunion disputes, which has worked with some degree of success.

Unlike the United States there was little "breakaway" or "dual" unionism, though an attempt was made, after the General Strike, to develop a "nonpolitical" Miners Union. This survived, mainly in South Wales, where the South Wales Miners Federation took as one of their tasks its elimination as soon as possible. The Union petered out in 1938. The only other attempt grew out of the discontent felt by the London Busmen at the allegedly bureaucratic Transport Union. A "breakaway" took place in 1937 and a small union survived for a few years without much effect.

The Transport and General Workers typified the trend towards large-scale unionism. After the merger with the Workers' Union with its 400,000 members it became the world's largest union. Bevin explained his recruitment policy at the 1927 Congress of the TUC, "In one town I organize the midwives, and in another the gravediggers, and everything between is the Transport Workers."

The comparative industrial and political peace of the thirties underlines the stability of British institutions. The Depression plunged whole towns and areas into mass suffering with the figure of unemployment for Wales being over 30 percent for the five years 1931–1935. The figure for Great Britain was just over 20 percent for three years, 1931–1933. In this period a large section of the people lived in poverty and squalor. Sir John Boyd Orr estimated that 10 percent of the population (with 20 percent of the nation's children) was poorly fed and some 50 percent of the people badly fed. In spite of the comments on Boyd Orr's sampling and statistics there is no doubt that his conclusions were broadly true. In some parts of Great Britain the slums were among the worst of any civilized country. In spite of these factors, the British workers on the whole remained unmoved by the fierce discussion in the labor movement over reform and revolution, the need to seize state power, the policy to adopt in event of a capitalist revolution, which went on in the 1930s between Strachey, Laski and Cole on one hand and Evan Durbin, Dalton and the young Fabians (Gaitskell, Crossman, Jay) on the other. The choice was unequivocally for reform and the gradualist, moderate policies put forward by the TUC and the Labour Party.

The thirties saw the rebuilding of this moderate labor policy after the 1920s model had broken down under the strain of rival and conflicting philosophies, Syndicalism, Guild Socialism, Revolutionary Unionism, Communism and Democratic Socialism. The events of the twenties and thirties saw a purging of some of those philosophies and the labor movement entered the year 1939 in spite of alarms, excursions and expulsions, more united in action and coherent in policy than they had been in twenty years. The TUC had grown from a small office with a few employees to a large building with several departments and an efficient secretariat. Its committees had more prestige and their decisions were reinforced by responsible trade unionism. One mark of this progress was the elevation, in 1940, of Ernest Bevin to the Ministry of Labour, a post he filled with distinction. Bevin's progress, in a sense, typified the changes in the British unions. The rebel of 1919, who led the dockers in their refusal to [load] arms to be used against the Russian Bolsheviks, became in time the architect of NATO.

III WORKING-CLASS LIFE

Anthony S. Wohl

WORKING-CLASS HOUSING IN NINETEENTH-CENTURY LONDON

Anthony S. Wohl is a member of the Department of History at Vassar College, but has also taught at the University of Leicester, England. He has published several articles on working-class housing in nineteenth-century London, and has edited an important contemporary source on the subject, The Bitter Cry of Outcast London. The excerpt which follows is drawn from an essay that appeared with seven other essays on working-class housing in various cities and regions of Britain, in a book edited by S. D. Chapman. The book is a welcome addition to the small body of scholarship on this important issue. Mr. Wohl's essay is particularly interesting because it is on London, it emphasizes the problem of overcrowding, and it highlights the equivocal role of housing and sanitary legislation, and the medical officers, in the problem. Mr. Wohl also points to the way out of the problem: cheap, rapid transport, leading to decentralization.

The pressure created by the rapidly multiplying population was greatly aggravated, especially in the central districts, by two factors —the necessity of many working men to live near their work, and the numerous displacements caused by various improvements and building. To live close to their employment was absolutely imperative for certain men: porters, market workers, men in the building trades, dock hands, tailors, jewelers (who often shared tools), and most of the casually employed. This necessity, of course, imposed a great burden upon house accommodation. "The crowding," wrote John Hollingshead in his *Ragged London in 1861,* "arises from the desire of the working population to be 'near their bread' as they express it; and the high rental of the tenements . . . arises naturally from this rush upon a particular spot. An empty room," he added, referring to Westminster, "is a novelty." In the 1880s almost one-half of those living in the dwellings of the Metropolitan Association for Improving the Dwellings of the Industrious Classes lived under one mile from their place of employment. A statistical survey, conducted by the London County Council's (LCC) Housing of the Working

From A. S. Wohl, "The Housing of the Working Classes in London, 1815–1914," in *The History of Working Class Housing,* edited by S. D. Chapman (Newton Abbot, 1971), pp. 16–31. Reprinted by permission of David & Charles Ltd. Footnotes omitted.

121

Classes Committee just before World War I, revealed that in Bethnal
Green, Southwark, Westminster and Holborn, a large number of working men gave their reason for enduring the high rents as "conven-
ience to their work." Even at this late date, when transport facilities
were much improved, over 24 percent of the total wage-earning
population of Bethnal Green had to live near their work; in Westminster the percentage was as high'as 40 percent (due to the large number of costermongers, hawkers, office cleaners and charwomen living
there); in Holborn 21 percent; and in Southwark, 25 percent. For
these men the suburbs were of little use: "I might as well go to
America as go to the suburbs," one casually employed workman told
the Select Committee on Artisans' Dwellings in 1882. Thus centered
around the great food markets, the docks, railways, workshops, and
homes of the wealthy were great aggregations of working-class
dwellings. It is important to notice in this connection that one urban
historian has recently defined the slum as representing "the presence of a market for local casual labor." Lower food prices, better
work opportunities for women and children, easy credit at local pawnshop or pub, and sense of community and tradition also served to
make many centrally located working-class families less mobile than
reformers would have liked.

The second factor complicating the housing problem in central
London was the continual dislocation caused by street, commercial,
and railway building. The social costs, measured in terms of higher
rents and lower standards, of the transformation of central London
into commercial and financial areas, were enormous, and go far to
explain why overcrowded conditions prevailed right through this
period. The activities of the railway companies in pushing their lines
through, and building their terminals in central London attracted the
greatest attention and probably created the greatest amount of dis-
placement and hardship. Ultimately, of course, the trains helped to
relieve central congestion by transporting thousands of workers to
the suburbs, but railway construction wrought such havoc that one
must conclude that in human costs the railways were responsible
for as much harm as good. So many houses were torn down during
the railway boom, which lasted down to 1867 and picked up again
after 1875, that contemporaries likened the coming of the railways
to the invasion of the Huns. Although the companies were required
to rehouse those displaced, they were easily able to evade their obli-

gations, and thousands were evicted in central London without any provision being made for their rehousing. In the 1870s, for example, the whole of Somers Town, a densely populated working-class district, was torn down to make way for the railway construction north of St. Pancras. Despite the protests of such groups as the Somers Town Defence League, the working classes were helpless in the face of the onslaught. In fact, in a period when men somewhat naively, but understandably, rejoiced in anything that assisted the demolition and aeration of dense slums, railways were often regarded as the panacea to solve the housing question. They were viewed as a double blessing, cutting through the slums and whisking the evicted inhabitants off to the fresher air, lower rents and higher morality of suburban living. Thus they were permitted throughout the nineteenth century to continue their construction with the minimum of effective interference from Parliament.

Adding to house demolitions in central London was a rash of commercial, street, and school-board building, and other improvements. Many of the wide new thoroughfares cut through working-class districts: Farringdon Street, Southwark Street, New Cannon Street, New Oxford Street, Commercial Street, Bethnal Green Rd, Wapping High Street, Clerkenwell Rd, Holborn, and Queen Victoria Street, all cut their way through rookeries. As with the railways, so with the new street building, contemporaries were generally more aware of the fact that disgusting eyesores were being torn down than they were of the social costs to the unfortunate inhabitants of the demolished buildings. A great number did in fact suffer eviction: New Oxford Street displaced some 5,000 people, Farringdon Street 40,000, and the construction of Holborn Viaduct, the Embankment, the Law Courts, the enlargement of Smithfield, and the docks (completed in the main by mid-century) all added to the pressure upon housing in neighboring districts. Of the fifty improvement schemes carried out by the Metropolitan Board of Works only thirteen provided for rehousing. Though the great damage done by the conversion of the City into a place exclusively of commerce and finance, and by street and railway building, took place largely before the 1880s, improvements continued to lead to demolition and evictions. The London County Council estimated that in the period between 1902 and 1913 over 45,000 rooms in central London and some 70,000 working-class rooms throughout London were destroyed to make way for various "improvements," and of these only 15,073 rooms were demolished to make way for new working-class dwellings.

The immediate result of this wholesale demolition and eviction was not the broad dispersion throughout London of the working classes, so much hoped for by reformers, but (due largely to the need to live near their work) increased crowding together in adjoining areas. Paradoxically, sanitary and housing legislation resulted in a similar undesirable increase in density of population in streets adjoining those recently demolished. The Torrens Act, 1868, which gave local authorities the power to demolish individual unsanitary houses, and the Cross Act, 1875, which extended the power to large areas, often aggravated rather than alleviated overcrowding. Pushed out from their homes and unable to move far afield or afford the rents of the model dwellings that arose on the sites cleared under the Cross Act by the Metropolitan Board of Works, the evicted thronged into the already crowded back streets and courtways, where, until the next round of slum clearance or street building, they remained in densely crowded dwellings. "I came to London twenty-five years ago," one poor woman told an East End clergyman, "and I have never lived in any room more than two years yet: they always say they want to pull the house down to build dwellings for poor people, but," she complained, "I've never got into one yet."

Had the sanitary acts been vigorously enforced, there can be little doubt that great discomfort and overcrowding would have resulted. Perhaps somewhat fortunately, it was largely up to the local medical officers of health to recommend the demolition of unsanitary houses to the vestries, and although these local bodies generally needed little encouragement to be inactive, it was more due to the sensitivity of the medical officers than to vestry apathy that the Torrens and Cross Acts were not employed more vigorously. For similar reasons legislation against overcrowding was not enforced, for medical officers were extremely reluctant to intiate any proceedings which might result in eviction without provision for rehousing. Clerkenwell, for example, was a vestry with a justifiably bad reputation for inactivity and overfondness of economy, yet the medical officer in his report for 1862 gave as the most pressing reason for not interfering with overcrowding and unsanitary dwellings: "if the occupation of rooms throughout the district were regulated, there would not be sufficient accommodation for the inhabitants." If to so many contemporaries the slum problem could be solved by the wholesale sweeping away of rookeries, those more informed attacked purely destructive legislation. The medical officer of health for St. Marylebone argued that to the working classes "sanitary improvement is a very car of juggernaut, pretty to look at, but which crushes them. Not a house is rebuilt, not an area cleared, but their possibilities of existence are diminished, their livings made dearer and harder." Had the Torrens and Cross Acts been used thoroughly, he continued, "an appalling amount of misery, of overcrowding, and of poverty would have been the result," and voicing an opinion common to medical officers, he concluded that "until tenements are built in proportion to those demolished at low rents, it is not humane to press on large schemes."

Thus while the great improvements and slum-clearance schemes carried out by the Metropolitan Board of Works certainly destroyed the infamous and fever-ridden courts and alleys of central London (such as St. Giles, Clare Market, and Wild's Rents), they did little to solve the housing problem. "All improvements recoiled on the poor," one medical officer sadly proclaimed in 1883, echoing the discovery, a few years earlier, by the special Charity Organisation Society's Committee on the Housing of the Working Classes, that "all social changes must tell first and most heavily, on the poorer classes." The correlation between the increasing density of people per house in certain central London districts, and demolition in or near those districts is very close indeed, and the impact of demographic pressures and house demolition upon working-class housing standards may be calculated from the fact that only seven of the twenty-nine registration districts of London witnessed a decrease in person-to-house density between 1851 and 1881. As the festering slums were slowly torn down, so the population became more compressed.

But throughout much of the nineteenth century, and certainly during the first half century, overcrowding attracted less attention than sanitary problems. Until the 1880s the housing question was seen largely in the light of broader problems of general public health. Descriptions of working-class housing in the early part of Victoria's reign are uniform in their portrayal of filth, stench and inadequate water and sanitary facilities. The local Committee of Health and

Sanitary Improvement, describing a street in central Westminster at mid-century, presented a picture which could be multiplied a thousandfold throughout London:

> *Although there is a sewer, the houses are not drained into it, but into cesspools, in surrounding premises. The rooms are crammed with occupants, irrespective of number, age, or sex, are most horridly dirty, as is also the scanty furniture, and many of the houses are very dilapidated, and without a semblance of ventilation. The cisterns or water butts are NEVER cleaned out; front kitchens, without any areas at all, are used as dwellings; the houses are let and underlet two, three, four times deep; and the privies are so filthily dirty on floors and seats as to prohibit their natural use and at the south-end of the street are large premises filled with cows on the basement and upper floors, from which the stench at times is unendurable. None of the houses are provided with ashbins, and such are the filthy habits of the inhabitants that the street would be impassable, but for the daily cleaning of it by the scavengers.*

The report concluded, perhaps not surprisingly, that "the morality of the inmates is unfortunately on a level with its sanitary conditions." The first reaction of many sanitary officials on entering the dwellings of the poor was to force, or even break open the windows and try to relieve their heaving stomachs with the comparatively fresh outside air. Visitors to working-class homes often commented on the boarded up or shut windows. While health enthusiasts and housing reformers like Octavia Hill advocated thorough ventilation, the undernourished inhabitants of unheated rooms had different ideas about fresh air. In addition to the lack of furniture (for much of the century "furnished" laborers' dwellings had only a few broken sticks), total lack of decoration and color, peeling walls, overflowing privies, rickety stairs, and blocked drains; contemporary descriptions stressed the fetid atmosphere and stench of the houses in which the laborers and poorer artisans were forced to crowd. Smell is one of the many intangibles with which the social historian of this period must deal. Victorians, well used to the heady odors of street and stable, repeatedly commented upon it. John Hollingshead, whose *Ragged London in 1861,* is one of the most accurate and compelling descriptions of working-class London, could hardly bring himself to enter some of the houses. "The stench throughout the house," he wrote of one dwelling off Regent Street, "although the front and back doors were wide open, was almost sickening; and when a room-door was opened this stench came out in gusts."

The miserable and dangerous sanitary condition of working-class tenements was not confined to the homes of the casually employed or poorer type of laborer, but applied also to the dwellings of thousands of skilled artisans, who, despite regular employment, sober habits, and adherence to the precepts of Smilesian self-help, were forced by the housing shortage to live, more often than not, in just one room in wretchedly unsanitary surroundings. Nor were the fever-nests to be found only in the relatively obscure alleys and by-ways of Whitechapel, Ratcliff, Shadwell, Poplar, Limehouse, Rotherhithe, and Southwark. Dickens, Hollingshead, Cardinal Wiseman (who first popularized the word "slum") and others pointed out that Westminster and the West End had some of the worst slums in London, and one writer correctly pointed out that "from Belgravia to Bloomsbury —from St. Pancras to Bayswater—there is hardly a settlement of leading residences that has not its particular colony of ill-housed poor hanging on to its skirts."

The poorly-built sewers, the irregular supply of fresh water, the lack of toilet facilities, and the density both of houses and people, made keeping a clean home a most arduous task during most of the first half of the nineteenth century, but certainly the habits of the very poor did nothing to assist general sanitary standards. While medical officers and sanitary officials were often sympathetic towards the plight of the poor, they were quick to condemn their behavior. "When these poorer people, especially the laborers, enter a house, at once begins a course of dirt and destruction," wrote the Clerkenwell medical officer in 1883. He continued:

The locks and handles of doors become toys for the children, and are soon demolished. The drain taps are sold at the bone and bottle shops, those left are never kept on; the closets are stopped up and the pans are broken. The chimneys are never swept, so that the rooms become blackened and disfigured. The paper is torn off the walls; the floors and passages are never washed, and there are no mats, so that the whole place becomes a mass of dirt and destruction. The water-butt lids and the dust-bin lids are used for firewood, the ball-cocks are broken off, so that there is great water-waste which floods the yards and washes away the cement from the paving.

The very hand-rails of the staircases are broken away and even the walls are picked with nails, or something of the kind so as to leave large holes. The windows are constantly broken and stopped up with brown paper; in fact, there exists in every parish a juvenile window-

breaking club, the members of which demolish every pane of glass they can, especially in empty houses.

Little wonder that so many argued that it was the pig which made the sty, and not *vice versa.* Many placed the best chance of an improvement in housing conditions in compulsory education; certainly as the century progressed working-class habits improved, partly in response to better sanitary facilities and to lessons learned in hygiene classes in school, partly as a consequence of increasingly strict enforcement of the nuisance removal and other sanitary acts.

The annual reports of the local medical officers of health and sanitary inspectors reveal a clear picture of slowly improving sanitary conditions. One must admire, and wonder at, the energy and determination of these officials who, in the face of great hostility from all sides (landlords, tenants, slum-owning vestrymen and ratepayers), went about their task with such grim enthusiasm. The number of annual inspections conducted by the local authorities was remarkable, a testimony to Victorian energy. The improvement in the sanitary condition of working-class homes was hindered, however, by the reluctance of so many local authorities to take advantage of the power to place tenements on a register, control them by strict by-laws and place them under a system of regular inspections, and by the inadequate number of sanitary officials for the ever-expanding population.

Nevertheless improvements were made constantly, although what the cost to the poor was, in increased rent, it is difficult to say. Certainly the opposition of tenants to sanitary improvements indicates where the cost often fell. As late as the 1890s it is clear that the enforcement of sanitary standards in the homes of the working classes presented a constant battle against petty offenses. Taking at random, for example, the annual report of the Mansion House Council's dwellings committee (one of several bodies assisting local authorities in spotting and correcting sanitary abuses) for 1894, there is a steady stream of complaints about drinking cisterns without covers, imperfect taps, bad gulleys, poorly-paved yards, defective drainage, wcs [waterclosets] cut off from the water supply, overcrowded conditions, inadequate dustbins, dangerous or defective brickwork, illegally occupied dwellings (attics and cellars primarily), and dangerous roofs.

In the face of such persistent sanitary defects, so often of a seemingly petty nature and so often leading to arguments over ultimate responsibilities and ownership, the quiet optimism of sanitary officials was quite remarkable. After years of aiding and activating local authorities, the Mansion House Council on the Dwellings of the Working Classes concluded at the end of the century that its labors had been rewarded with "a fruitful record of victories achieved in a quiet, unobtrusive way and without sensationalism. . . ." All the available evidence points to a steady improvement in sanitary conditions throughout working-class London. It was not due to the advance in medical science alone that the working-class quarters of central London were, by the last quarter of the nineteenth century, no longer feared as fever-breeding haunts of depravity and contagion.

Unlike the problem of sanitary defects, the problem of overcrowding became more serious as the century wore on. By 1885 the Royal Commission on the Housing of the Working Classes was quite correct to stress in its *First Report* that overcrowding was "a central evil around which most of the others group themselves." Lord Shaftesbury's evidence before the Commission, based upon sixty years' experience, that "overcrowding has become more serious than it ever was," was corroborated by almost all witnesses. Statistics of overcrowding and person-to-house density are always misleading, for both landlord and tenants had very good reasons for concealing the amount of subletting, and most local authorities were extremely reluctant, for a variety of reasons, to employ night inspections. Behind the bare figures of an increase in person-to-house density from 7.03 (1801) to 7.72 (1851) to 7.85 (1881), there is a clearly discernible trend towards overcrowding, which reached an extremely critical and dangerous level in the 1880s. By 1896 London's person-to-house density had reached 8.02, the highest of the century. The LCC for statistical purposes considered more than two persons to each room to constitute overcrowding. By this measure, in 1896, over 56,000 one-roomed tenements, over 55,000 two-roomed tenements, over 24,000 three-roomed tenements, and nearly 10,000 four-roomed tenements were overcrowded; out of a total of 632,148 tenements, 145,844 were considered overcrowded. These figures represent all London, and all classes; the figures for working-class houses would reveal an even greater amount of density and distress.

Overcrowding was certainly increasing both in intensity and in extent throughout London up to at least the census year 1891. After that there is contradictory evidence, but overcrowding did not significantly increase, and probably decreased somewhat, between 1891 and World War I. During this period significant decreases in overcrowding took place in the densely populated central districts—Holborn, St. Marylebone, Westminster and the City of London. The four most crowded working-class districts of central and eastern London (Shoreditch, Finsbury, Bethnal Green and Stepney) all experienced a decline in overcrowding between 1891 and 1911. Taking the percentage of inhabitants living in one- to four-roomed tenements who were living in overcrowded conditions, we get the following figures for 1891, 1901 and 1911 respectively: Shoreditch, 43.9 percent, 39.7, and 36.6; Finsbury, 52.4, 45.6, and 39.8; Bethnal Green, 45.0, 38.9 and 33.2; and Stepney, 45.3, 47.4 and 35.0. Taking London as a whole, the respective percentages of overcrowding (for those living in one- to four-roomed tenements) were: 35.5, 29.6, and 17.8. Between 1891 and 1901 overcrowding decreased in every metropolitan borough within the County of London except Stepney; but over the next decade overcrowding in central London districts appeared to increase again, and in only eight boroughs (Chelsea, Hampstead, Holborn, St. Marylebone, St. Pancras, Stepney, Westminster and Woolwich) did overcrowding decrease between 1901 and 1911. The degree of high-density living was still staggeringly high in the early twentieth century. In 1911, of the single-roomed tenements in London, 43.8 percent were overcrowded, and of the two-roomed, 41.3 percent: in Stepney, Bethnal Green, Shoreditch, St. Pancras, St. Marylebone, and Southwark, over 30 percent of the population were living in one- or two-roomed tenements, while in Holborn and Finsbury the percentage was over 40.

As overcrowding in London increased, so too, naturally, did the rents. Rents had always taken a large slice out of the workingman's wages and constituted, with food, the largest item in his budget. The Royal Commission on the Housing of the Working Classes discovered in the course of its comprehensive investigations that the London artisan and laborer classes were spending much too much on much too little. Over 85 percent of the working classes paid over one-fifth of their income in rent, and almost one-half paid between one-quarter and a half. After the Commission's Report in 1885 rents began to rise even more steeply than before, and proved to be the great exception to the general trend of falling prices during the late-nineteenth-century "great depression." The price of accommodation thus held back whatever gains in real wages those working men who remained steadily employed were able to make in the last two decades of Victoria's reign. In the East End accommodation was so difficult to find that a system of key money was introduced, making still further demands on the workmen's pocket.

Whereas in the 1850s 2s 6d for a single room was the average rent in central London, by the 1880s it had crept up to 4s 9d or so, and the cost of two rooms—7s 6d to 10s was often beyond even a semi-skilled artisan's wages. One observer, complaining about the lack of single rooms for under 4s in Kensington and Lambeth, cautioned that "rents of less than six shillings a week are generally danger-signals, unless the amount is for a single room." "The chief item of every poor budget," she added, "is rent. . . ." Official figures for London in 1905 revealed a clear pattern of steeply rising rent for houses with a gross annual value of £50 and under. Taking the year 1900 as the base year of 100, working-class rents rose in the following manner: 1880 (87), 1885 (92), 1890 (90), 1895 (96).

As rents soared so the cry for fair rents, first raised after the 1881 Irish Land Act, became more prevalent. Not only did left-wing groups, such as the Social Democratic Federation, press for fair-rent tribunals, but several medical officers of health took up the demand, and the Hackney Borough Council asked the other borough councils to join it in pressuring the government to apply the Irish Land Act to London. *Justice,* which frequently criticized the apathetic attitude of the London working man to his surroundings, felt that the increase in rents might achieve some good, for it might drive tenants to demand better, more sanitary, accommodation and awaken him from his political stupor. The medical officers were uncomfortably aware that the sanitary legislation they were enforcing was pushing up rents, and in 1883 their president, Dr. Dudfield, argued that "he could not free his mind from the belief that before this question was solved there would have to be fixity of fair rent."

The high rents were the product, primarily, of the relentless pressure of people upon houses, and the increasing costs of land and house building. The medical officer for Hackney, disturbed by the alarming rent rise of 33 percent in his area between 1894 and 1901, produced figures which revealed that in Hackney the cost of

building materials had increased by 40 percent, and that of labor
by 18 percent between 1880 and 1900. Summarizing his research
we get the following figures:

1880–1900

Materials	Average Increase (Percent)	Labor	Average Increase (Percent)
Bricks	39	Bricklayer	16
Timber	30	Carpenter	16
Lead	54	Plasterer	16
Iron	80	Plumber	16
Stone	27	Painter	14
Lime	30	General Laborer	30
Cement	20		
Average	40	Average	18

If the hours worked per week are taken into account, bricklayers in
1914 were earning about 8s 6d more per week than in 1873, and
laborers about 8s per week more. In the London County Council's
experience, brickwork rose from £11 per rod in 1890 to £20 15s
per rod in 1898, and, in the same period iron and steel rose 20 percent and laborer's wages 27 percent. Combined with new building
regulations, these costs made it extremely difficult for even the model
dwelling companies and trusts, operating on a dividend of 3 percent to 5 percent, to build blocks of dwellings in central London
which could be let at rents the working man could afford. To these
costs must be added the inability of housing interests to compete
with business and commercial interests for centrally situated land.
Land in central London became so expensive as to make the building of working-class housing there an almost impossible task. The
Metropolitan Association for Improving the Dwellings of the Industrious Classes had spent about £41 per room at mid-century;
by 1881 the cost of its buildings worked out at over £60 per room.
The London County Council's Boundary Street Scheme in the East
End worked out at between £67 and £79 per room, and if the baths,
bakery, clubrooms and workshops are included the cost was over
£90 per room.

Given rising costs of land, materials and labor, and more stringent building codes, it is small wonder that little large-scale working-class house construction was undertaken in central London after the 1880s. By 1890, of the model dwelling companies, only the Peabody Fund was pursuing a policy of extensive building, and although it was joined by the Sutton and the Guinness Trust, and many new, impressively well constructed, blocks went up in Westminster, Chelsea, and other central districts, the overall total of rooms provided by the philanthropic societies down to 1914 was not impressive, and generally the rents were such that only the better-paid artisans could afford them. In 1905 the *Economic Journal* was forced to observe that

> *the increased cost of building, due partly to greater expense in labor, material, and land, but also to the far higher standard of house accommodation required by modern hygienic laws, had made it almost impossible for the ordinary builder to provide dwellings at low rents.*

Faced with the realities of rising costs, two alternatives, partly complementary, suggested themselves: to encourage the natural movement of the population from central London to the suburbs where land values and building costs were lower and to accept the tendency for London to subdivide itself into heavily concentrated commercial and residential areas; and, for those who could not be encouraged by cheap transport and lower rents to move into the suburbs, to provide housing in central London through the various local authorities or the central London government. Suburbs or subsidized housing appeared to be the only solutions to an overwhelmingly difficult housing situation.

The infinitely cheaper land outside the built-up areas of the metropolis presented an opportunity to develop large working-class estates, if only cheap transport facilities could be provided. As early as 1857 the *City Press,* acknowledging economic realities, argued that overcrowding would never be conquered so long as there was an insistence upon building in central London. "Cannot some plan be devised," it inquired, "for bringing the suburbs nearer to the metropolis? We mean, of course, by railways." In the 50s and 60s pleas for "suburban villages" or "railway villages" connected by radial arms to a continuous railway belt round London were frequently raised. Working men occasionally joined in the cry: "Why don't they build us a great village or town out Epping Way . . . and then let the railways bring us backwards and forwards for a trifle. They take our homes; let them give us something in return."

In fact, not until the Cheap Trains Act of 1883 were the railway companies compelled to give "something in return." Before this Act there were several companies running workmen's trains, either because they were discovered to be profitable, or because special train acts required their use. Nevertheless, before 1883 the number of working men carried by trains to the suburbs was negligible. In 1882 only 25,671 tickets were issued daily to workmen. After 1883 the number of workmen's trains increased, although not as fast as housing reformers would have liked. Railway companies were still able to evade their statutory obligations, but from 1883 onwards constant pressure was put upon the companies to provide a more effective, thorough, and extensive service. Of several pressure groups, the National Association for the Extension of Workmen's Trains, a group with several left-wing affiliations, was the most powerful. Its president, George Dew, was also a member of the LCC's Housing Committee, and partly under Dew's guidance, the LCC strongly supported the demand for an extension of transport facilities to the suburbs.

The central London government kept up constant pressure upon the railway companies and Board of Trade, and it was in more or less permanent session with the railway companies, negotiating an extension (both of time and distance) of workmen's trains which would be acceptable to the railway board and other interested parties. By steady pressure, but partly as a natural consequence of the great growth of the suburban population, which made workmen's trains more of a paying proposition, the number of workmen's tickets issued daily greatly increased from the 26,000 issued just before the 1883 Act. By 1902 almost 325,000 daily tickets were issued, and while in 1883 there were only 106 workmen's trains running daily in London for a total distance of 735 miles, in 1897 there were 466 such trains (3,248 miles), and by 1914, 1,966 workmen's trains, covering 14,060 total miles. Equally instrumental in opening up the suburbs, was the rapid development of an efficient, if somewhat slow, tram service. The Board of Trade in 1908 discovered that the best and cheapest facilities from the center to the suburbs were provided by the South London electric tram system. As early as 1884 the chairman of the London Tramways Company, which served South London, calculated that accommodation for 20,000 people had been provided along its routes and, he argued, his company had "relieved London of an immense number of poor people" by carrying them out to the suburbs. John Burns, the President of the Local Government Board, argued in 1907 that "the taking of the tramways over Westminster and Vauxhall Bridge did more to open up the minds of the industrial classes of the big city than twenty-five years' previous housing agitation."

The vast improvement in transport facilities greatly assisted the development of the suburbs, although it is extremely difficult to correlate exactly the development of any particular area and workmen's transport facilities to that area. As early as 1852 Dickens, lamenting the invasion of London by "Brigadier Bricks" and "Field Marshal Mortar," drew attention to the fact that "in no part of London is the invasion . . . so perceptible as on the line of railways. . . ." The astounding growth of working-class suburbs after 1850 (between 1851 and 1891 Willesden leapt from under 3,000 people to over 114,000; West Ham from under 19,000 to over 267,000, and Leyton from under 5,000 to over 98,000) was certainly facilitated by the availability of cheap and rapid transport. Although as Dr. Dyos has shown, the suburbs began to build up their own corporate identities, and were becoming self-sufficient communities which were attracting workers from both central and extra-London areas, the suburbs were still essentially dormitory communities, dependent upon good communications with various parts of central London. The connection between working-class suburban growth and cheap transport may be seen in the case of North East London, which attracted many more working men, and grew far more rapidly, than the western or southern suburbs, largely because of the policies of the Great Eastern Company, which provided the most comprehensive service of workmen's trains. At the end of the century, the Valuer of the LCC, speaking for that body's housing committee, commented:

The Great Eastern Railway Company . . . is the only company which offers reasonable facilities for the travel of the working class; and the result is that ever-increasing numbers of the working-class population are practically forced along the lines of the Great Eastern Railway; so that while there is an enormous working-class population in that one direction, there are, in the north, west, and south of London, within a much less distance from the Bank of England, large tracts of land not developed for the erection of houses—sometimes within the county boundaries.

The LCC's statistical office pointed out that of all the working-class rooms built during the years 1902 to 1908 well over one-third were situated in the northeastern suburbs.

Michael Anderson

WORKING-CLASS FAMILIES DURING THE INDUSTRIAL REVOLUTION

Michael Anderson of the University of Edinburgh, Scotland, is another scholar who has added to our knowledge of an aspect of working-class life that had either been ignored or treated in accordance with ideological considerations. He has studied the effects of urbanization and industrialization on the working-class family in Preston, a Lancashire industrial town. Using census data from Preston and from rural communities that sent migrants to the city— as well as other sources—he has been able to show that there was some breakdown in family ties in the city, particularly among young, unmarried people. However, he stresses that most families maintained their ties to relations, and one-quarter of the households contained relatives. They did so primarily for support and help in times of crisis. In the excerpt, Mr. Anderson shows how certain critical life situations fostered family cohesion.

. . . I have suggested that in nineteenth-century Lancashire most members of the resident urban working class over the age of about 18 were able, if forced or wishing to, to obtain and hold down a job, to find a home, and to obtain satisfaction of most day-to-day domestic needs, without the assistance of family or kin. Those with family and kin assistance could, it is true, often obtain jobs, home, and domestic life which would give them somewhat more satisfactions than they could otherwise have obtained. These somewhat marginal advantages fail, however, at the structural level, to explain why such a large proportion of the old (who often could not render even these services) were apparently supported by their children. They fail to explain why assistance was so often given to siblings and to other kin, notably orphans and widows, who were also unable to help in these ways, or, indeed, in the short run in many cases to render any real service at all. They fail to explain why so many married couples should wish to live with or so near to their parents. Nor, I have argued, does it seem likely that normative factors can have any very great independent role, except possibly to reinforce pressures resulting from elsewhere within the system.

The resident urban class in nineteenth-century towns, above all in the rapidly expanding factory towns of Lancashire, were thus not crucially dependent on others for some of the basic needs of life—a home, work, and the company of others. In this chapter, however, I want to argue that they still needed various other kinds of help at sufficiently regular intervals to make them in great need of some reasonably predictable and regular form of assistance.

Every family in all societies faces from time to time what I have here called critical life situations. Sickness, unemployment, death, or disaster remove the basis of the family's support, leave orphans and widows, require families to make temporary or permanent arrangements for the substitution of roles, cause worry and distress. Old age, marriage, and childbirth, too, all frequently mean that those undergoing them are in need of help. Finally, there are many pressing day-to-day problems; finding someone to care for the baby while the wife works, someone to look after the key while one is out, someone from whom to borrow some small amount of a necessary item of food when the supply suddenly and unexpectedly runs out.

In mid-twentieth-century Western industrial societies, the more serious critical life situations occur only rather rarely for each individual family, and their worst financial and welfare consequences have been somewhat moderated by the impact of the welfare state or other bureaucratic source of provision, or forestalled for most families by insurances of various kinds. Moreover, as the standard of living of the mass of the population has gradually risen, the economic impact of all forms of contingency has become somewhat less pressing.

Under these circumstances, help from nonbureaucratized sources of assistance—neighbors, friends, and kin—of a kind which demands a considerable expense of time and effort, is only absolutely necessary in rare cases, in what Litwak has called idiosyncratic events, where there are gaps in the bureaucratized provision, or where this becomes temporarily overloaded.

In nineteenth-century towns, on the other hand, not only were these major crises more frequent, but bureaucratized means of assistance were either inadequate, or provided only at the cost of serious concomitant deprivations which tended to some extent to cancel out the benefits received. Moreover, I shall argue here that of the nonbureaucratic sources of support only the family had a framework within which reciprocation could occur which was sufficiently clearly defined to provide an adequate guarantee of assistance in the major crisis situations. It was thus advisable, or even well-nigh essential, for kinsman to make every effort to keep in contact with and to enter into reciprocal assistance with kinsman, if life chances were not to be seriously imperiled.

Bureaucratized Forms of Assistance

. . . Most of the people under study here lived at times below or near to the primary poverty line, and few had any substantial savings to fall back on in time of crisis. Under these circumstances, any happening that removed, even for a short time, a person or family's means of support was potentially very serious indeed. For the person without any other form of assistance the only universal bureaucratized form of help was the Poor Law. Some also could use friendly society benefits where available.

However, there is considerable evidence to suggest that, in Lancashire, the Poor Law was seen by the mass of the population only as a refuge of last resort. This phenomenal definition seems to have coincided, moreover, with what an assessment at the structural level would lead one to conclude. Comment is widespread to the effect that few Lancashire operatives could swallow their pride and submit to the degradation, as they saw it, of appearing before the Guardians and being interrogated about their family means: "The much dreaded workhouse." "I'd as soon ha' gone to prison as do it . . . just go up there before the Board,—see what they thinks of poverty there; then, maybe, you'll know why we working men had rather clem (starve) than trouble them." "Descending to the pauper rank, a fate which the operative class generally regards with a repugnance somewhat morbid! Almost invariably they speak of the workhouse as the 'Bastille,' and to be taunted as a 'pauper' would be by many regarded as the most opprobrious of epithets."

There is also evidence to suggest that when the operatives said that they would rather starve, they meant it nearly literally. Almost all seem to have made every effort to try any and all alternatives, before making an application. It was well known that the Lancashire poor rates were the lowest in the country except in times of severest distress (and even then they were below average), though higher wages, favorable population age compositions, and low unemployment helped here. Nevertheless, surveys both at the beginning and the end of the century found lower pauperism among the old than the national average, even though employment for old men and old women was not easily obtained.

Also crucial, however, in a population composed largely of migrants, was the fact that migrants could often not obtain relief in the community where they and their families were at the time living. They had a "legal settlement" elsewhere, and only there did they have any legal right to receive relief. The able-bodied could often in spells of temporary distress obtain relief in the town though they had no legal right to do so. But large numbers of widows and of aged and infirm persons and their families were periodically removed to the town or village of their birth. The Irish, most of whom had no legal settlement in England, were even more reluctant to apply, for removal for them meant being dumped in any Irish port often far from their birthplaces, where anyway they might well not have lived for twenty or more years.

Poor relief was, then, for most, a last resort because of the extreme dissatisfactions it brought with it. Friendly society membership, on the other hand, was widespread among the Lancashire proletariat, even more widespread indeed than among the rest of the population of England. It seems probable that by the early 1870s rather over 420,000 out of a Lancashire population of 2.8 million were members of friendly societies proper and almost a million more were making payments to burial societies. In other words, rather over half of all adult males were insured in friendly societies, and about half the population were insured in burial or friendly societies.

These are fairly impressive figures, even taking account of the fact that they mean that half of the population, the richest but also most of the very poorest, were not covered. On the other hand the benefits of friendly society membership, though important, were limited. Few friendly societies paid anything for crises other than sickness and death of the insured and his wife. The payments for sickness, 6s to 13s (usually 7s to 10s) were only one-third to one-half of the already inadequate average wage, and even these usually only continued for about six weeks before they fell to a lower rate of (normally) half the full figure. Death benefits were up to about £10, but that was all a widow could usually expect. Thus, while these societies undoubtedly helped to alleviate the suffering of sickness and bereavement, and kept many off the Poor Law for a time, even these crises were still times of severe economic deprivation. Moreover, the human problems remained largely unmet. So, too, did the other critical life situations—old age, unemployment, childbirth, migration.

The rest of this chapter will examine a number of these critical life situations, and will attempt to investigate the part played by the different alternatives to the formal agencies in meeting them.

The Young Married Couple, and the Old

The first set of critical life situations which I shall examine involves the problems facing, on the one hand, the young married couple, and, on the other, the widowed and the old, and the linkages which emerge between them. It seems, in fact, that people phenomenally perceived this as a sphere where the maintenance of relationships led to a mutual increase of satisfactions in the form of fairly short-run and instrumental returns, regardless of other considerations, and that the prospect of these mutually advantageous returns was an important factor in the retention of the relationships.

. . . In the first years of marriage few couples, particularly among the lower paid, lived in a home of their own. Most of those who could live with parents did so, the rest living instead in lodgings. In the later stages of the life-cycle, most couples headed their own households. Some of these, however, had parents living with them (some 4 percent in LCS's 3–5), and others lived only a short way away from their parents. Table I shows that in all no fewer than 32 percent of old people aged 65 and over lived with a married or widowed child, and a further 36 percent with unmarried children.

Stehouwer found that about three-quarters of the population of 65 and over in the three modern Western countries which he studied

TABLE I

Residence Patterns of Persons Aged 65 and Over, by Sex, Listed in Priority Ordering, and Excluding Those in Institutions: Preston Sample, 1851

	Males %	Females %	All %
Living:			
with married child	31	33	32
with other child	38	34	36
with spouse	17	10	13
with other kin	—	10	5
as lodger	11	3	7
as servant	—	3	2
with no other person	3	8	6
All: %	100	101	101
N	93	101	194

had at least one living child. A calculation was made on the basis of assumed mortality rates and marriage ages, which suggested that only some 67 percent of the persons of 65 and over in the Preston sample would have been in this position had they been a random sample of the population. There is obviously some margin for error in this latter figure, but it does certainly suggest very strongly that there were few old people who could not find one among their children prepared to give them house room in old age, if they actually had any children alive.

. . . Few households contained two married couples of two succeeding generations. It was thus, above all, widowed parents who actually shared with married children. This is clear from Table II.

Thus, it was above all the fact of being widowed and alone, rather than old age itself, which was crucial in leading to co-residence of married children and parents. These widowed persons were almost all old people who either had no income of their own, or had only a very much reduced one. Some were undoubtedly becoming rather infirm. For them the advantages of the arrangement are obvious enough.

Apparent advantages to the couples can be summed up under four heads:

1. . . . A strong relationship between family size and whether or not couples headed their own household. Saving of rent seems to have

TABLE II

**Residence Patterns of Persons Aged 65 and Over, by Sex and
Marital Status, Listed in Priority Ordering, and Excluding Those
in Institutions: Preston Sample, 1851**

	Widowed		Married	
	Male %	Female %	Male %	Female %
Living:				
with married child	50	41	15	17
with other child	27	34	50	42
with spouse	..	..	35	41
with other kin	—	10	..	..
as lodger	18	4	..	..
as servant	—	3	..	..
in other residence patterns	5	7	..	..
All living with children	77	75	65	59
All: %	100	99	100	100
N	44	70	46	24

The difference between the proportion of married old people living with married children, and the proportion of widowed old people in this position is significant $p < 0.001$ (chi^2 = 16.351). This group is, however, somewhat older, so this is in part to be expected, but widowed persons were also significantly more likely to be living with any kind of child, in spite of their greater age ($p < 0.05$ on a one-tailed test; chi^2 = 3.831).

been of crucial importance here. Rents for a whole cottage started at 2s 6d per week. The couple would also, if both worked, have had considerable difficulty in doing their housework, washing, and cooking, and might well have had to pay something further for this. In lodgings these latter problems were solved, though at a price, and rent was perhaps only 1s 6d or 2s per week. Sharing with kin meant, however, that this sum would instead have gone into the family purse to the mutual advantage of parents and kin. The best statement of this motive for sharing with parents though in this case stressing the economic advantage to parents is to be found in the *Report on the Condition of Frame-Work Knitters,* where a Leicester framework knitter noted that he went to live with his wife's parents "because they could not afford 2s 6d a week for a house."

2. Operatives married young. Few seem to have had many savings. They were thus unable to buy even the minimal scraps of fur-

niture necessary for a home of their own. Sharing or lodging helped them solve this problem too.

3. Germani noted that housing shortages were an important factor encouraging co-residence with parents by young married couples in Buenos Aires. No direct evidence on this point emerged from the descriptive material, but the very considerable housing shortage in Preston and the other cotton towns was noted [earlier]. . . . Even if these couples had wanted a house of their own they would have had some difficulty in finding one.

4. . . . Although many mothers worked, many of them had their mothers or other relatives available at home to care for their children in their absence.

I would argue that one explanation of the large number of stem families noted by Foster in Oldham when compared with the other towns he studied may well be that married children were only too willing to take in parents or other kin who were prepared to perform this service and thus allow the mother to work. When, later, their families became too large to make actual co-residence possible, the possibility of obtaining this assistance seems likely to have been a strong inducement to married children to live nearby. Some sources suggest that it cost up to 3s 6d or even 5s to pay a nurse for a week, though these higher figures usually included the cost of some kind of feeding. Even if the net cost were 1s 6d, probably a minimum, a parent or other unemployed relative living in the house and performing this service was making an important contribution towards her keep, and this was increased if she also saved the family from the need to pay someone to do the cooking. Table III does show, moreover, that if there was a grandmother in the house, the mother was significantly more likely to maximize her earnings by working away from home.

Twenty-nine percent of those with a grandmother in the house and children under 10 worked, and 58 percent did not work at all. Of those with no grandmother or other nonemployed person in the house, the figures were 12 percent and 76 percent respectively. These figures are highly suggestive of some link between grandmothers, child care, and working mothers. In part, however, this link may be one of co-variance rather than causation. The proportion of mothers who worked fell over the life-cycle, and so too, as the parents died, did the number of married couples with co-residing

TABLE III
**Relationship between the Employment of Mothers and the
Co-residence of Nonemployed Grandmothers and Other Persons:
All Mothers with Children under 10, Preston Sample, 1851**

	Mother works:			Mother does not work %
	in factory[a] %	elsewhere, place uncertain %	at home %	
Household contains:				
co-residing grandmother	16	11	5	5
co-residing other person	31	27	23	22
no co-residing other person	54	62	72	73
All: %	101	100	100	100
N	84	37	43	482

[a] It is never possible to be absolutely certain about where mothers worked, so these allocations may contain a very small amount of (presumably random) error, which actually works against the hypothesis and thus makes the trend shown here, if anything, an underestimate.

parents. So also, however, to some extent, did the proportion of couples with a child under 10. Unfortunately, any further breakdown of these figures reduces the values in some of the cells so much that no conclusions of any validity can possibly be drawn. It may however be noted that the proportion of working mothers fell particularly sharply in LCS's 3 and 4. In these LCS's, poverty was, however, at its worst, so one could at least hypothesize that mothers were forced to stop working in these LCS's just because there was no longer a grandmother available to care for the children. A much larger sample would be necessary to test these suggestions.

Clearly, then, the quantitative data can take the argument no further. The proposition gains added support, however, from the descriptive data. Firstly, . . . there is much evidence that children were frequently left with kin and friends, both those living in the house and those living nearby.

Secondly, there is evidence that the exchange element in this element of the parent–married child relationship was valued and recognized. Indeed, a number of cases appear where it is consciously cast into money terms.

The most clear-cut case of this exchange evaluation is cited by Waugh, and does not actually refer to a relative at all. He refers to a household which contained, besides a family with an infant child whose mother worked, an old lady of 70 who "was no relation to them, but she nursed, and looked after the house for them. 'They cannot afford to pay me nought,' continued she; 'but aw fare as they fare'n, and they dunnot want to part wi'me. Aw'm not good to mich, but aw can manage what they wanten, yo see'n.' " "It is very common," said another commentator, "that when a young man and woman marry they have parents, and that they may both work in the mill, they get one of their mothers to keep house." Sometimes, indeed, payment was actually made for this service even to kin. The young married son of a Parish Assisted Migrant and his wife had had a home of their own in Princes Risborough. When they got to Staleybridge, however, he and his wife moved in with his family of orientation and are noted as paying 3s per week to them "towards the rent, for house room and nursing the child."

It was, moreover, precisely this exchange argument that was put forward as one explanation of Lancashire's low poor rates. "Even the aged members of a manufacturing community have a different social position from that of the same class of persons in many of the parts of England. . . . Many . . . , especially aged females, afford a service very appropriate to their condition, and of not inconsiderable value, by keeping house and taking care of the youngest children, while the working part of the family are absent at their work. . . . With such assistance in the care of her household, during her absence at the factory, many an industrious married woman is enabled to add 8s, 10s, or 12s weekly to the income brought in by her husband and the elder of her children. It is not uncommon for aged females to become domesticated for the purpose of affording service of this nature in the families of those who have no elderly relatives to support."

The ability of old women to perform these services seems, then, to have been of great importance. It was even noted that "elderly persons . . . come with their children, who support them, and they take care of the house, and cook." It would seem that for migrants to bring in parents to help them out in this way may not have been a rare phenomenon.

In this connection I also made a comparison between the proportion of old people on relief in Lancashire and the proportion in other industrial and mining communities with similar proportions of persons in the 15–64 age group on relief but where there was little employment for married women, using data prepared by Booth on the situation at the end of the century. This analysis did indeed suggest very strongly that, either because they were able to support themselves better, or because they were supported for the reasons outlined above, old women (though not old men) were much less likely to be on poor relief in Lancashire than elsewhere. The same appeared to be true also for other areas where women were habitually employed away from home.

The feeling that parents who were supported should make some specific reciprocal contribution to the family's finances comes out in other ways too. Thus "I took the beer-house, thinking as my father and mother-in-law had nothing to do, they might make a little by selling beer." This family was also dependent on the mother-in-law for caring for the children, for the wife was a cripple, and so the mother-in-law's death was "the worst shock I had ever experienced." A number of cases also appear where support was willingly given to dependent parents, but only on the condition that the Poor Law authorities provided some assistance also.

In sum, it does seem that in Lancashire towns married couples and their parents could often each maximize their satisfactions by engaging in relationships with each other, that these mutual advantages were specifically appreciated by both parties, and that this was an important factor in the maintenance of these relationships.

Michael Young and Peter Willmott

WORKING-CLASS FAMILIES IN THE SUBURBS

Long before Michael Anderson analyzed the working-class family in the nineteenth century, sociologists Michael Young and Peter Willmott had studied it in the 1950s. In fact, it was Young and Willmott, joint directors of the Institute for Community Studies, who originally "discovered" what has come to be known as the traditional pattern of working-class kinship (in Britain). This pattern or network is characterized by a day-to-day exchange of mutual aid and is built around daily contacts between mothers and their married daughters. Young and Willmott documented the network by means of intensive interviews in an old working-class ghetto, Bethnal Green in East London. Then they moved to a new working-class housing estate, to which they gave the fictitious name Greenleigh. There they pursued the same methods—and found that the traditional network broke down in the suburbs. Some of their findings are included in this excerpt.

Once the family moves to the housing estate, the question of how they came to be there has for them an academic flavor, and for us the question now is the difference migration has made to them. Table I compares contacts with relatives before leaving Bethnal Green with those in 1953 and 1955. It records the *total* contacts of husbands and wives with parents and siblings on both sides: before he moved, the average husband, for example, saw one or other of his relatives on fifteen occasions in a week.

As one would expect, people saw very much less of relatives after moving to the estate. Some relatives, of course, if they already lived on the estate, were seen more often, but the general effect of this was slight, since under one-twentieth of all parents and siblings (18 out of 382) were on the estate even by 1955. Most relatives were seen less after the move. To reveal what difference this made we must rely on the accounts given in the interviews. Mr. and Mrs. Harper were one of the couples. Before their move, they led the kind of life we have described in the first part of this book. The contrast between old and new has been sharp.

From Michael Young and Peter Willmott, *Family and Kinship in East London* (London, 1962), pp. 131–142. Reprinted by permission of Routledge & Kegan Paul Ltd., and the Humanities Press, Inc.

TABLE I
Changes in Weekly Contacts with Relatives after Migration
(Greenleigh sample—39 husbands and 41 wives)

	Average number of contacts per week with own and spouse's parents and siblings		
	Before leaving Bethnal Green	Greenleigh 1953	Greenleigh 1955
Husbands	15.0	3.8	3.3
Wives	17.2	3.0	2.4

Mrs. Harper, a stout, red-faced woman in her late thirties, had, like her husband, always lived in the same part of Bethnal Green before she went to Greenleigh in 1948. She came from a large family— six girls and two boys—and she grew up amidst brothers and sisters, uncles and aunts and cousins. When she married at eighteen, she went on living with her parents, and her first child was brought up more by her mother than by herself. As the family grew, they moved out to three rooms on the ground floor of a house in the next street. Their life was still that of the extended family. "All my family lived round Denby Street," said Mrs. Harper, "and we were always in and out of each other's houses." When she went to the shops she called in on her mother "to see if she wanted any errands." Every day she dropped in on one sister or another and saw a niece or an aunt at the market or the corner shop. Her many long-standing acquaintance-ships were constantly being renewed. People were always dropping in on Mrs. Harper. "I used to have them all in," she told us, "relations and friends as well." At her confinements, "all my sisters and the neighbors used to help. My sisters used to come in and make a cup of tea and that." And every Saturday and Sunday night there was a family party at Mrs. Harper's mother's place: "We all used to meet there week-ends. We always took the kiddies along."

That busy sociable life is now a memory. Shopping in the mornings amidst the chromium and tiles of the Parade is a lonely business compared with the familiar faces and sights of the old street market. The evenings are quieter too: "It's the television most nights and the garden in the summer." Mrs. Harper knew no one when she arrived at Greenleigh, and her efforts to make friends have not been very successful: "I tried getting friendly with the woman next door but one," she explained, "but it didn't work." It is the loneliness she dislikes most—and the "quietness" which she thinks will in time "send people off their heads."

Her husband is of a different mind. "It's not bad here," he says. "Anyway, we've got a decent house with a garden, that's the main thing—and it's made all the difference to the children. I don't let the other people here get me down." He still works in Bethnal Green—there are no jobs for upholsterers at Greenleigh. This has its drawbacks, especially the fares and the time spent traveling, but it means he is able to look in on his parents once a week and call about once a month on his wife's father and eldest sister—Mrs. Harper's mother having died, "the old man lives with Fanny."

Mrs. Harper herself seldom sees her relatives any more. She goes to Bethnal Green only five or six times a year, when one of her elder sisters organizes a family party "for Dad." "It costs so much to travel up there," she said, "that I don't recognize some of the children, they're growing so fast." Tired of mooching around an empty house all day, waiting for her husband and children to return, with no one to talk to and with the neighbors "snobbish" and "spiteful," Mrs. Harper has taken a part-time job. "If I didn't go to work, I'd get melancholic." Her verdict on Greenleigh—"It's like being in a box to die out here."

Mrs. Harper's story shows how great can be the change for a woman who moves from a place where the family is linked to relatives, neighbors, and friends in a web of intimate relationships to a place where she may talk to no one, apart from the children, from the moment her husband leaves for work in the morning until he comes home again, tired out by the journey, at seven or eight at night. It is not just that she sees less of relatives than before: as a day-to-day affair, as something around which her domestic economy is organized, her life arranged, the extended family has ceased to exist. Other women remarked on their sense of loss. "When I first came I felt I had done a crime," said Mrs. Prince, "it was so bare. I felt terrible and I used to pop back to see Mum two or three times a week." "It's your family, that's what you miss. If you're with your family, you've always got someone to help you. I do miss my family," "We do miss the relatives out here," "I miss my Mum," others told us in similar vein.

The loss was not so keen for all. One took her mother with her, another her husband's mother, two had sisters on the estate. But for most of the women the move meant a sharp break with the full life they had previously shared with others. For example, when they lived in Bethnal Green, twenty-four of the forty-one wives had seen one or more women relatives daily: at Greenleigh in 1955 only three did so.

After Two Years

One reason for interviewing migrants on two occasions—with a two-year interval between—was to allow us to see how the family's relations with kin were altered by the passage of time. In quantitative terms, the average drop in contacts between 1953 and 1955, shown in Table I, is slight. But behind the averages lie some changes for individual families which are worth reporting.

On the one hand, by 1955 some families saw more than they had done two years before of relatives who had since joined them on the estate. An example is Mrs. Trent. Her parents-in-law moved to Green-leigh between the two phases of interviewing, and she saw her mother-in-law three times a week instead of once in three months.

On the other hand, some women had "settled down" at Greenleigh in the two years and had loosened their ties with their old homes. One thing we noticed in 1953 was that six of the women were still continuing to shop in Bethnal Green as often as once a week. Food was still rationed then and they had not broken their registrations with the shops they knew so well in Bethnal Green. If they went to Bethnal Green to shop, they could see relatives at the same time. By 1955 only one of the wives was going up to Bethnal Green on a regular weekly shopping expedition, though others went occasionally to get clothing and other things cheaper there. "I don't go up there for shopping now," said Mrs. Clive, "not now we've got our own shopping center here." The effect this can have on meetings with kin was voiced by Mrs. Rawson—"I haven't seen my Aunt Ada for a long time. We used to be rationed in Bethnal Green and then I used to see her occasionally in the market, but not now."

These women had gradually become less absorbed in Bethnal Green and more in Greenleigh. The Maggs family illustrates what "settling down" can mean. In 1953 they described themselves as "lodging" in Greenleigh; Mr. and Mrs. Maggs both went to London to work and their daughters (like a few other children in 1953, but none in 1955) to their old schools in London; now Mrs. Maggs has had another child and is at home all day, while one of her daughters expects to be coming to work at the local glassworks as soon as it opens. Though Mrs. Maggs says she feels "lonely" and "misses her relations," they are lodgers at Greenleigh no longer.

One link has not been broken by time—many of the husbands have continued to work in London. At Greenleigh there are local jobs in only a limited number of trades. There are few openings for tailors, cabinet makers, french polishers, dockers, or lorry drivers. In 1953, thirteen of the forty-seven husbands were working in the East End and a further nine in other parts of the County of London; by 1955 some individuals had changed one way or the other, and there were by then fifteen out of thirty-nine working in the East End and eight elsewhere in London. From the estate as a whole, more people were traveling to the East End in 1955 than in 1953.

Since many men have to travel to the East End for their work, their contacts with relatives have in general fallen less since they moved to the estate than their wives'. The husband has to meet his fares out of an income already strained by the higher rent. But if he has to pay his fares anyway, he can not only get to work on the one ticket but to his relatives also, and in some ways their very presence at the other end of the line may relieve his daily journey. Mr. Mallows finishes his work in Bethnal Green at five. At that time "the guards are forcing people into those trains every night," so he goes to his father's, to have a cup of tea. When he has finished that and had a chat, the rush-hour is over; there is even a chance of getting a seat. Mr. Parker used to go home every day for his dinner before he moved to Greenleigh. He cannot get used to the sandwiches which he takes instead, so he often has a hot meal at home with his mother. He has to pay her but at least that is cheaper than any other way of getting a hot dinner. Other men still make a point, as they did in Bethnal Green, of calling each week on their mothers, or they see their fathers and brothers at work, or just "bang into" uncles and aunts and cousins on their walk from tube station to workplace, or in their dinner break.

They do not keep up with their own relatives alone; they do so with their in-laws also. Mr. Ellis, who works in Bow, visits his wife's mother regularly once a month. Mr. Lowie works in Bethnal Green as a cabinet maker and has his midday meal every day with his wife's sister. Other husbands call regularly to pay into family clubs, more often run by their wives' relatives than their own. Mr. and Mrs. Adams belong to a Public House Loan Club, and Mr. Adams "calls in on a Friday to give my sister our Club money. She takes it and pays it in for us."

In 1955, six of the forty-one wives were working in London also. Mr. Marsh had been working in a shop in Bethnal Green in 1953 and had kept in touch with the relatives, particularly his own mother; by 1955 he had got a job in a shop at Greenleigh instead, but now his wife was working for London Transport. "Being on the buses," he pointed out, "the wife sees her mother and my mother more than I do now."

It is not so much the distance that makes visiting difficult for the other women as the cost. Time and again, wives lamented that they were so short of money that they could not afford to visit Bethnal Green as often as they would like. "If the fares were cheaper you could afford to go more often and it wouldn't be so bad," was Mrs. Adams's verdict. "The fares put the damper on visiting relations more than anything else."

The New Pattern of Visiting

Even so, few women were cut off entirely. If we exclude the mother actually living with her daughter at Greenleigh, the twenty wives whose mothers were alive were, in 1955, still seeing them on average just under once a fortnight. Mrs. Young, although she does not like going back to London at all because she feels shut in and choked there, goes about once a month all the same because "with your family it's only natural, you've got to see them."

Visiting between relatives is sometimes a two-way affair. Migration can be something in which the kindred share, the house and garden belonging not only to the family who live in it, but also in a sense to their relatives as well. Mrs. Soper, one of our Bethnal Green informants, said that every fortnight she takes her two children "on the Underground down to my sister at Hainault. We have a nice afternoon out there. It's quite a little outing." Mrs. Berry's sister also appreciates the attractions of Greenleigh: "She loves to come down here. She says it's better than going to Southend or somewhere like that." But you don't go to Southend in the winter. When the days begin to draw in and the morning air is colder, so too is enthusiasm for an excursion to the windswept spaces of a housing estate. "It's really a bit of an outing for them to come out here in the summer time," Mr. Parker explained, "but we see all the relatives less in winter than in summer."

In summer the most popular time for visiting is, of course, the weekend. On a Sunday morning in the summer dozens of people can be seen coming out of the station, many carrying bags of fruit and flowers, as one person said "quite like hospital on a visiting day." "Last August Bank Holiday," said Mrs. Hall, "we had fourteen relatives down here." Visitors do not necessarily stay for only one day. Greenleigh is suitable for holidays as well as day excursions. Sometimes people told us, as Mrs. Lowie did, "Mum comes down to stay two or three times a year." In Bethnal Green, the kindred are at hand every day of the week. At Greenleigh the family has to wait for summer, for weekends, for holidays, before they appear. But people still feel themselves members of the wider family, reaffirm their membership of it when they attend family rituals like weddings, funerals, and Christmas parties "back home," and use key relatives to keep them informed. "I go to see the wife's sister every week," said Mr. Vince who works in Bow, "to find out if there are any messages or anything about other relatives." Such roundabout communication with the families of origin is probably all the more necessary to husbands and wives who now spend so much time on their own.

The approach we have adopted so far in this chapter—looking mainly at changes in *contacts* with relatives—is only one way of measuring the impact of the move. Another approach is to inquire about *services,* to ask what help the family gets on the housing estate compared with Bethnal Green. What happens, for instance, when the family faces extra problems—when the wife is incapacitated by illness or confinement?

Care in Illness

Even those Greenleigh wives whose homes had not been visited by sickness had considered the prospect with misgiving. If husbands were away from work their families had to make do on a small sickness benefit, sometimes paid tardily at that.

> Last year my husband was off work and the health money took ages to come down. I told the rent collector and he said "That's no excuse."

"Well, what am I to do," says I, "the health money's not come down. You know how long it always takes out here." Then on top of it all if I didn't have a saucy letter from them saying I'd missed a week's rent. It's above the limit, isn't it?

Families with savings exhausted them. Families without had to borrow from relatives. The Todds would have been in an even worse state without help from the wife's father.

When we first came my husband got ill with shingles. Because of the moving there was a muddle-up over the panel money and we didn't get it for four weeks. So we had to borrow from my father and give everything up in order to pay the rent. On top of that there was the funeral money we had to borrow because when we first came we had to cash in all the insurance policies he had when he was ill and so we didn't get any money for the baby's funeral. We had to pay back father for that as well as the rest he lent us.

When the husband was ill, his wife looked after him. When the wife was ill, who looked after her? We asked wives at Greenleigh, as in Bethnal Green, who was the main person helping them with the home and children, when they were last ill in bed. At Greenleigh there was, of course, less help from relatives. Of the twenty-four Bethnal Green wives who had been ill, twelve had been helped during their sickness by relatives, eight of them by their mothers; but of the twenty-one wives at Greenleigh who had been ill since going there, only four had help from relatives, two from their mothers. One of these two was Mrs. Chortle whose mother was living with her; the other was Mrs. Windle, who was ill in bed for three days with tonsillitis. "I stayed off the first day to look after the children. Then I couldn't stay off any longer," said her husband. "So I phoned up a neighbor in Wembley to tell her Mum. She came down for the next two days and stayed. It didn't cost her much because she had a privilege ticket, Dad being on the railway." Mrs. Tonks's sister also came down when she was ill. The other wife who received help got it from her aunt living on the estate.

If relatives were too far away, who did it instead? Four people out of the twenty-one at Greenleigh (compared with four out of the twenty-four in Bethnal Green) had help from neighbors, six from husbands. Husbands might have done more but for the fear of losing the wages which were all the more needed in time of illness. The consequences could be serious if they did.

> *My husband had to stop away from work when I was taken ill last time. He went to the Assistance Board and they said if you're still out in four weeks come back again. We'll never go there again. It was the first time we needed money and still we didn't get any back for all we'd paid in. Bet's club (a family club in Bethnal Green) is better; you can depend on that.*

At all costs he had to bring in the money.

> *My husband lost three days but then he had to go back because we couldn't do without the money. The doctor said I was supposed to stay in bed a week but I had to get up. I got an abscess in the breast because I got up too soon.*

In Bethnal Green, people with relatives close by seldom go short of money in a crisis like this. If they do not belong to a family club from which they can draw a loan, some relative will lend them money. Borrowing from relatives is often more difficult at Greenleigh. "You notice the difference out here," said Mr. Tonks, "when you fall on hard times. Up there you were where you were born. You could always get helped by your family. You didn't even have to ask them—they'd help you out of trouble straight away. Down here you've had it." "That's why families stick together," said a Bethnal Green husband. "If you're short of money you can always go round your Mum and get helped out."

At Greenleigh the shortage of money drives the men back to work —leaving the responsibility to the children. The main difference between the two places was that wives depended more on their children —seven out of twenty-one were looked after by them, as compared with two out of twenty-four at Bethnal Green. "When I was ill, my eldest daughter stayed at home from work and looked after me," said Mrs. Berry, and her husband confessed his own helplessness when he added, "When Mum's ill, Dad's ill as well, you know what I mean? I wasn't a bit of use myself; I don't know how we'd have managed if it hadn't been for Shirley."

Children younger than Shirley stayed away, not from work, but from school. When Mrs. Painswick went to hospital her eldest daughter, then aged eleven, stopped at home to look after her younger brother and sister. Her aunt visited the home to see if everything was all right and afterwards came to the hospital to report that her daughter was managing very well—"everything was spotlessly clean." Even so Mrs. Painswick worried continuously. Mrs. Rawson suffered too.

> *I got such a chill through leaving off my underslip that I nearly took the cow's way out. I had to keep Billy back from school. I broke down having to do that. Billy did the shopping and paid the rent man and I struggled to do the cooking.*

The question about help at childbirth showed the same decline in dependence on relatives. Of the wives at Greenleigh, nineteen had had their last child since they moved to the estate, and Table II com-

TABLE II
Care of Children at Last Confinement (Marriage Samples Compared)

Person caring for older child(ren)	Bethnal Green sample	Greenleigh sample
Relatives	29	4
Husbands, children, or neighbors	15	15
Total	44	19

The Bethnal Green total excludes one family in which the only other child was ill in hospital at the time of confinement. The Greenleigh total is of all the wives who had been confined since their arrival on the estate.

pares the help given to them at their confinement with that given to the wives in the Bethnal Green sample. We asked who looked after the older child or children while the wife was confined, whether this was at home or in hospital.

The kindred of Bethnal Green were no longer predominant. Out of the twenty-nine wives in Bethnal Green helped by relatives at their confinement, eighteen were helped by their mothers: at Greenleigh only one wife was—the Mrs. Chortle whose mother lives with her. Of the remaining three relatives, two were living at Greenleigh, and one came out to stay. Of the other fifteen families, neighbors helped only five; one family turned to a Home Help; seven husbands stayed off work; and in two families the children looked after themselves.

In day-to-day affairs, too, neighbors rather rarely took the place of kin. A few wives said they went to the shops with another woman, or that they got errands for each other, or that they took turns at fetching the children from school. The more usual reaction was like that of Mrs. Todd, who complained, "When the baby was ill, not a soul knocked at my door to get me an errand." Even where neighbors were willing to assist, people were apparently reluctant to depend on them too much or confide in them too freely. Mrs. Hall, although she was helped by a neighbor at her recent confinement, said, "I don't think you can go to a neighbor if you want anything personal." Mrs. Maggs said, "If I'm ill she comes in and looks after the baby but it don't do to visit, does it?" "My husband," said Mrs. Young, "doesn't think it right to have neighbors in the place."

Robert P. Neuman
WORKING-CLASS SEXUALITY

Robert P. Neuman, who teaches at State University College in Fredonia, New York, is one of the very few historians who have studied human sexuality. He has studied lower-class sexuality in Imperial Germany. Unlike his predecessors, he does not portray urban workers' sexual practices as significantly less "moral" than those of agricultural laborers. Citing statistical and autobiographical evidence, he suggests that premarital affairs were common to both groups. The only difference was that in rural areas, these affairs usually led to marriage, whereas in the city they could lead to prostitution. Mr. Neuman does not attribute the difference, as earlier observers and historians did, solely to the impact of industrialization. Instead, he argues that the key to the difference—and the decline of traditional morality—lies in the secularization and rationalization of society.

There seems to be an assumption that factory and urban life stimulated an increase in illegitimate births during the nineteenth century. This increase might be interpreted as the result of changing and presumably "looser" codes of premarital behavior. It is not possible here to examine in detail this cause-and-effect relationship, riddled

From R. P. Neuman, "Industrialization and Sexual Behavior: Some Aspects of Working Class Life in Imperial Germany." Reprinted by permission of the publisher, from *Robert J. Bezucha: Modern European Social History* (Lexington, Mass: D. C. Heath and Company, 1972), pp. 283–291. Footnotes omitted.

as it is with demographic and semantic problems. Rather we can better approach the subject of illegitimate births at that time with the help of some contemporary German statistics on illegitimacy, leaving aside for the moment the question of morality.

We can begin by comparing the illegitimacy rates of what can be called urban and rural areas. In 1900, the number of illegitimate children (that is, those born to unmarried women, a rather unsophisticated but common definition) born in German cities with populations of 2,000 and more was 9.14 per 100 live births, while that of smaller towns and the countryside averaged 6.16 per 100. With just this data, it might be argued that there was some causal relationship between city life and illegitimacy. But these raw figures are deceptive. It is significant, for example, that the illegitimacy rate in the Rhineland-Westphalia industrial region as a whole was only 4 percent between 1896 and 1900, a fact partly attributable to the higher ratio of men to women living and working there. Thus in a region where one might expect to see most clearly the "loosening" effect of industrial and urban life on morality as indicated by illegitimacy, we find a level more than two percentage points lower than in the countryside. Admittedly, it is difficult to distinguish between "urban" and "rural" simply by town size and the presence of a few large factories. Also, it is possible that by 1895 the most unsettling effects of industrialization were beginning to fade while newer, more stable patterns of sexual life were established.

Some evidence that these patterns were "leveling out" in the three decades after 1867 emerges from a study of the fecundity rate (the ratio of those women who actually have children to all women in the population between the ages of fifteen and fifty). An examination of the period from 1867 to 1897 reveals that the fecundity rate of married women (like the actual numbers of marriages) appears to fluctuate roughly in accord with economic conditions. However, the fecundity rate of unmarried women, which supposedly should increase during this period of German social and economic transition and expansion, remains very nearly constant (see Table I).

In general, these figures simply indicate that the illegitimate fecundity rate does not seem to be as closely tied to economic changes as the legitimate rate, a point already noted by earlier social historians. At present, nothing conclusive can be said about the relationship between industrialism, urbanization, and illegitimacy. Nevertheless,

TABLE I
Fecundity Rate of Married and Unmarried German Women,
1867–1897

	Number of Live Births to Every 100 Married Women between Ages 15 and 50		Number of Live Births to Every 100 Unmarried Women between Ages 15 and 50	
Years	Germany	Prussia	Germany	Prussia
1867–1871	. . .	27.3	. . .	2.47
1872–1875	29.7	30.0	2.90	2.49
1879–1882	27.4	28.8	2.98	2.61
1889–1892	26.5	27.2	2.83	2.51
1894–1897	26.7	26.9	2.92	2.48

it must be stressed that the traditional view of illegitimacy as one of the outstanding characteristics of urban sexual life cannot be accepted without a good many qualifications.

Turning from these quantitative measurements back to the autobiographers, we find indications that the sexual behavior of the urban working classes may not have differed radically from those of agrarian workers. Citing the farmhand Franz Rehbein's autobiography, Adelbert Koch concludes that "a false impression prevails about the influence of village morality. Among agricultural workers, intercourse with the other sex is as free as among factory workers." For example, Rehbein noted the same kind of overcrowded living conditions among farm workers that was once given as a cause for the looser sexual morality of urban workers. Furthermore, Rehbein describes an event that took place on a large Pomeranian estate where he worked as a fourteen-year-old that lends support for the German adage *Ländlich, Schändlich* (literally, rural = shameful). At the close of the potato harvest the farm workers, men and women alike, celebrate a "potato marriage." In a scene reminiscent of a Breughel painting, the workers provide their own music with fiddle and harmonica, while couples disappear from time to time into the haylofts and stalls of the barns. All of this seems to take place in an atmosphere of peasant exuberance unmarked by any twinges of conscience.

Later, while working as a hired hand on a farm in Holstein, Rehbein started courting Dora, a servant on a neighboring farm. Unable to marry, according to Rehbein, because of his low wages, he began to make nightly visits to his sweetheart, where "the bedroom window of my Dora was not obstructed by a nasty lattice." Rehbein got into the habit of spending the night with Dora and then returning to his job early the next morning. This went on for nearly a year. Then, when Rehbein was twenty-six, Dora became pregnant. Marriage, which earlier seemed out of the question for economic reasons, suddenly became imperative. Dora and Franz married just a month before the birth of their first child.

Rehbein's account lends some support to the impression that sexual intercourse between men and women intending to marry one another was a common occurrence in the countryside. In a survey conducted by the Evangelical Church's Morality League in the mid-1890s, approximately half of the women married in the country parishes were considered "fallen brides," which was usually, but not always, the same thing as unwed mothers. Referring to premarital intercourse, one pastor from Schleswig-Holstein remarked that it took place "sometimes after the public betrothal has taken place, sometimes before; the latter as frequently, yes, probably more frequently than the former."

Of course, this premarital behavior and Rehbein's experience may only have been representative of the sexual behavior of a certain group of farmhands. Nevertheless, Rehbein's premarital sex life and his manner of entering into marriage can be usefully compared with several other urban autobiographers. Like Rehbein, Moritz Bromme did not marry until his sweetheart became pregnant. He confesses that "if I hadn't got my 'bride' pregnant, I probably wouldn't have married for a long time." Wenzel Holek and his "wife" lived together "on trial" for seven years before deciding to get married and give their two children a "legal father." Eugen May also lived in a common-law arrangement, but for a much longer time. As May puts it, he had "provided" a girl for himself when he was seventeen in 1904. Seventeen years later he was able to announce in his autobiography that "we now intend, in the very near future, to finally get married." It would be going too far to conclude from these few examples that most working-class men in town and country only married after the intended wife became pregnant or after several years of living together. The autobiographies simply indicate that premarital sexual intercourse and common-law marriages were not at all unusual among factory and farm workers alike. Hence, it can be suggested that, in this sphere at least, men and women from both areas shared some common sexual behavior patterns.

Prostitution is another subject that can illuminate the similarities and differences between urban and rural sexual life. Although the world's "oldest profession" has been a common literary theme and many nineteenth-century reformers regarded it as *the* social evil, social historians have as yet given prostitution and its practitioners scant attention. This is not surprising, for prostitution, its nature, extent, and causes, is an extremely complex social and psychological phenomenon. Students of prostitution in the last century often took a simplistic view of the subject, attributing it to a decline in "morality" (a view popular with conservative social critics), poor wages for women in home and factory industries (the common socialist view), or innate mental degeneracy among certain women (the conclusion of Cesare Lombroso, the Italian criminologist). Today authorities on the subject give some weight to each of these factors and add to them a variety of psychological nuances involving the learning of sexual roles and the sexual experiences of women in childhood. In addition to these problems of interpretation, there is a shortage of reliable quantitative and qualitative data on nineteenth-century prostitutes, not to mention their customers. In spite of these difficulties it is time to begin a serious investigation of prostitution, for it leads into several interesting and hitherto little explored areas of the past. In the remarks that follow I rely on several contemporary studies prepared before the First World War.

Before we begin, however, the reader should understand that in Imperial Germany prostitution as such was not prohibited by law. Rather it was tolerated. That is, prostitutes were required to register themselves with the police in their place of residence. They were issued a special identification book, prohibited from living in or frequenting certain parts of the city, and expected to report for weekly or biweekly medical examinations. Those suspected of having a venereal disease were placed into hospital until "cured" and then they usually went back on the streets. Since these prostitutes lived under police control they were known as "supervised girls" (*Kontrollmädchen*). Although it seems clear that these *Kontrollmädchen* represented only a minortiy of the active prostitutes in most cities, it is from studies of them that we get our most reliable information.

In view of the extent of immigration from the countryside to urban centers in late nineteenth-century Germany, it is not surprising that less than half of the registered prostitutes were natives of the cities where they had lived and had usually lived there less than five years. This was the case with 2,224 Berlin prostitutes in 1872–1873 and also in Hamburg and Cologne early in the present century. It was often presumed (especially by socialists) that these *Kontrollmädchen* were predominantly farm girls who came to the big city seeking work as domestic servants, then were seduced by their masters (or master's son), and finally turned into the streets. Although it is true that a very high percentage of registered prostitutes gave domestic service as their former occupation, the romantic notion of the "daughter of the people" corrupted by the master of the house is not supported by the available evidence, which is not to say that it never happened. To begin with, not many *Kontrollmädchen* seem to have been from farm family backgrounds. If we use the occupation of the prostitute's father as a rough guide to social origins we find that about half of them came from artisan (that is, craftsmen like shoemakers, carpenters, plasterers, and the like) and factory backgrounds. Table II offers some general information on the occupational backgrounds of prostitutes' fathers, but it can only serve as a very rough guide owing to the imprecision with which various job categories were defined by officials and also incomplete knowledge of the geographical origins of the prostitutes themselves.

Although this information must be used cautiously, it does seem clear that not many daughters of farm owners or farm laborers became registered prostitutes. When they did, however, it is possible that they did so not after seduction by their social betters, but rather by carrying over into an urban setting their rural sexual code. It has been shown from the autobiographies of farm laborers that premarital sexual intercourse and lengthy "affairs" were not unheard of in the German countryside. What happened if a country girl came to the big city as a domestic servant (as so many did, having no other skills to offer), took a lover almost always from her own class background, and perhaps became pregnant? Back home on the farm she could expect to marry the child's father sooner or later. But in the city this solution was not nearly so certain. The servant girl might find herself without a job and with a child to support. Already an outcast in a society that condemned bastardy, such a girl might resort to prostitution.

TABLE II
Occupations of Fathers of Registered Prostitutes
(Percentage of Total)

Occupation	Berlin (1872–73)	Breslau (1901)	Frankfurt a. M. (1911)	Hamburg (1912)	Cologne (1913–14)
Artisans and craftsmen	47.9	72.0	33.0	22.2	30.0
Factory workers	22.0		20.0	30.6	12.8
Farm owners and workers	4.1	4.2	...	3.2	7.0
Miscellaneous and unknown	26.0	23.8	...	44.0	50.2

It is possible to compare the experience of these farm girls with that of the daughters of artisans and factory workers. Before doing so, it is worth noting that here it is difficult to differentiate clearly between urban and rural backgrounds, because many artisans and factory workers lived in towns of less than 2,000 people and might therefore be classed as rural. This is a problem that might be overcome by correlating a variety of factors concerning prostitutes (place of birth and its population size, parental occupation, and so forth), but for the purposes of this essay it will be assumed that artisans and factory workers can be defined as nonrural in the sense that they do not work on the land.

The high percentage of the daughters of artisans among *Kontrollmädchen* was interpreted by some contemporaries as an indication of the declining economic and social position of this social group in Imperial Germany. It should be understood that through most of the nineteenth century, German artisans considered themselves to be eminently respectable citizens, closer to the middle class than to the emerging factory proletariat. Certainly it is difficult to imagine a daughter of a puritanical, not to say prudish, German artisan of the late eighteenth century ever becoming a prostitute. After 1870, German artisans found that their once proud position was being undermined by the factory system. They could not always support their daughters at home until they married. It seems likely that the daughters of artisan fathers (particularly from small towns) moved to larger towns and cities looking for work as servants. The life stories of prostitutes from the nonrural artisan and factory backgrounds follow a common pattern, whereby girls drift into, rather than deliberately choose, prostitution as a way of life: the girl leaves school at fourteen without any skill in hand; within a year or so she takes a job as domestic servant, waitress, or barmaid, often in a location other than her home town; after another year she is going steady with a boy from her own social class, not infrequently someone from her own home town or even a distant relative; sexual relations begin casually, often after a few beers on the way home from a dance; the girl becomes pregnant, and for one reason or another, the boy friend refuses (or cannot afford) to make an "honest woman" of her; she has a child, who usually dies before his first birthday; the girl enters into a more permanent "relationship" with another man and becomes a semi-kept woman, that is, she may be living in common-law with a working-class man while she earns money as a barmaid, washerwoman, or other; this relationship eventually ends and the girl drifts into affairs more and more transitory until she finally decides to turn "professional" and registers herself as a prostitute with the police.

Are there any common factors here? One seems to be that the premarital affairs of rural areas could and usually did lead to marriage. In the countryside, social pressures could be brought to bear on a man who left a pregnant girl in the lurch. But the same kind of affairs in the city, with its increased anonymity and different moral codes, might gradually evolve into professional prostitution. In addition, prostitution among women from either urban or rural origins seems to have been the end point of a process more or less free from moral compunctions about premarital sexual intercourse. Again and again prostitutes recount their life stories with an air of innocence and matter-of-factness devoid of any qualms of conscience usually associated with traditional moral codes. It is perhaps the decline of the authority of these codes that is the key to the "loosening" of morality, sexual or otherwise, in the German working classes after 1870. Instead of talking about the "impact" of industrialization on working-class morality, the social historian might better regard changes in sexual attitudes and behavior as an integral part of the gradual secularization and rationalization of society already under way before Germany began its period of rapid industrialization after 1870.

Perhaps this theme can be enlarged and clarified by looking at the practice of contraception among the German working classes. That pregnancy was so frequently a forerunner of working-class marriage and part of the prostitute's evolution would seem to indicate ignorance and/or indifference about contraception in these classes. Information on this subject is now very sketchy, but with the help particularly of several hundred interviews conducted by Max Marcuse in 1917 on the nature and extent of contraception in working-class marriages, several points can be made.

First, contraception is rightly regarded as being a phenomenon associated with a rather well-developed stage of industrial and urban life. This seems to be true of Imperial Germany, although it must be emphasized that even in the 1890s a variety of folk and scientific methods of contraception was available to rural workers. Coitus interruptus, or withdrawal, was of course the most common, if the most unreliable, method for those who wished to prevent conception. "Rubber articles," probably condoms, were available in some rural areas, especially around larger towns and cities. Elsewhere mothers nursed their children up to age three in the hope of remaining infertile, while other women brewed up extracts of various barks and leaves for either contraception or abortion. Knowledge of more sophisticated and reliable means of contraception seems to have spread to the countryside through men returning from military service or from women returning from domestic service in the city, or even through advertisements in the popular press. Nevertheless, many people in the countryside continued to look upon a large family as "natural" and sometimes as a positive economic factor. Such people tended to regard contraception, even in the form of coitus interruptus, as a "citified" custom. Thus, in an interview in 1917, a twenty-nine-year-old North German farm laborer, the father of three (only one of which was still alive) declared that he and his wife did not practice birth control: "My wife is far too stupid for that. She doesn't understand it, and wouldn't want it at all. [I] also don't want it. It's not the fashion by us. They do that in the city." In spite of this attitude, the knowledge and practice of birth control seems to have spread perceptibly in rural Germany before 1914.

Secondly, the ability and the desire to limit the number of one's children, to regulate the interval between births, or to have no children at all are all indications of a sophisticated level of social, economic, and most important, intellectual development. The decision to use contraception indicates that the users are trying to exercise control over a part of their lives that traditionally lay beyond their control. As people become more conscious of their socioeconomic status, of their sense of individuality, and their chances for ego gratification they begin to rationalize and demystify their sexual lives with the help of contraception. Children are no longer the usual and often feared result of sexual intercourse. Pleasure rather than conception can become the aim of the intercourse. Those who use contraception with these aims in mind, even when efforts to prevent conception fail, are already breaking away from older, religious traditions. They are also showing that they believe that they can influence their own destiny in very significant ways. In the words of Lee Rainwater,

> a sense of stability about and trust in the future . . . is one precondition for consistent [family] planning. Closely related to this is the belief that one can affect one's future, can determine to some extent what will happen. . . . In addition . . . a person has to be able to assume that he can be effectively assertive in [the] world, and that he can mold the future closer to his heart's desire.

In keeping with these observations, in the working classes of Imperial Germany it appears to have been the better-paid, skilled industrial workers, many of whom held "advanced" or socialist views, who increasingly assumed that they could indeed assert influence over their lives and practiced birth control most effectively. So a thirty-four-year-old Berlin master mechanic, an agnostic married five years and with one child, said during an interview in 1917 that his wife used a diaphragm to limit births because "we want to get ahead and our daughter should have things better than my wife and sisters did." Among the autobiographers Moritz Bromme, an ardent Social Democrat and metal lathe operator, and Ludwig Tureck, Communist typesetter, speak of their desire and efforts to limit their family size so that they and their wives will be less vulnerable to economic privation. Another class-conscious worker, a thirty-seven-year-old Berlin factory foreman and father of three, told Max Marcuse during the First World War that coitus interruptus was the form of birth control used by him and his wife. The reason for doing so was because "a person owes it to his future to limit births. . . . We workers are no longer as stupid as before, when we supplied children for the rich and for the state—factory and cannon fodder—that doesn't go anymore, and if our wives ever go on a birth-strike [*Gebärstreik*] we'll see if everything doesn't get better." The point here being that contraception forms an integral part of a secularized, demystified world view held by some German workers.

The emergence and evolution of this secular world view is the positive way of expressing what is usually called the "demoralization" of the working classes. I have suggested that perhaps "demystification" might be a better descriptive term. It can be argued that what was once regarded as the demoralization of workers under the impact of industrialization and urbanization was really a part of and another stage in the decline of traditional religious and social sanctions that antedates the rapid changes of the post-1870 period. In negative terms German workers showed less respect for the old proscriptions against premarital sexual intercourse, illegitimacy, and contraception. In positive terms, within a social setting increasingly urbanized and industrialized, they developed a more secular set of standards stressing the enjoyment of this life rather than the next as well as a conscious desire to control and improve the conditions of their lives. It seems clear that in the years before 1914 the old religious beliefs and the growing secular concerns lived side by side in the world views of many working-class Germans. The process of demystification incorporating the decline of old traditions and the creation of new ones operated at different tempos in town and country. The visible manifestations of this process may only have become noticeable in the mushrooming cities of Imperial Germany. But to overemphasize the contrast between urban and rural sexual behavior and attitudes is to risk overlooking the common elements and the evolution of both.

Seen from another perspective, contraception and even prostitution in Imperial Germany can be interpreted as ways in which the working class responded to a social existence largely beyond its control. The prostitute has usually been regarded as a criminal, a threat to society; but she can also be interpreted as a woman rationally trying to relate to a socioeconomic system that, in Imperial Germany, offered few attractive positions to women. This is not to say that prostitution was the most sensible or appealing response to a variety of social controls; but it can be said that the prostitutes (and ordinary criminals too) may be usefully interpreted as people struggling to order and control their own lives in a highly structured and authoritarian society. Contraception seems to be a similar response. Together, prostitution and birth control, the archenemies of traditional sexual and moral codes in the last century, may, in the long view, be seen as two facets of the desire of "little people" to control their own lives.

Robert Roberts

WORKING-CLASS COMMUNITY

Robert Roberts is a scholar who has written on a number of topics. For our purpose, however, he is most interesting because he grew up in a famous working-class community, Salford, and wrote about that community in The Classic Slum. *Roberts is capable of analyses; he is also apt at vivid description. What stands out about his book (and the handful of other books written by educated children of workers) is the grasp and description of the complexities of working-class communities. Roberts is certainly aware of the great gulf between workers and middle class, but he does not belabor the point. Rather, he talks about the worker community as an entity unto itself. In the excerpt, he talks about community "caste" structure, social aspirations and attitudes. Some of his comments are more negative than those made by other educated children of the slums. This may be a reflection of the slum he grew up in, or it may derive from his refusal to pander to sentimentality.*

In our community, as in every other of its kind, each street had the usual social rating; one side or one end of that street might be classed higher than another. Weekly rents varied from 2s 6d for the back-to-back[1] to 4s 6d for a "two up and two down." End houses often had special status. Every family, too, had a tacit ranking, and

From Robert Roberts, *The Classic Slum* (Manchester, The Manchester University Press, 1971), pp. 4–16, by permission of the publishers. Footnotes omitted.

[1] Back-to-backs were a type of housing common to Northern English industrial cities. They were houses which shared a back wall in common.—Ed.

even individual members within it; neighbors would consider a daughter in one household as "dead common" while registering her sister as "refined," a word much in vogue. (Young women with incipient consumption were often thought "refined.") Class divisions were of the greatest consequence, though their implications remained unrealized: the many looked upon social and economic inequality as the law of nature. Division in our own society ranged from an élite at the peak, composed of the leading families, through recognized strata to a social base whose members one damned as the "lowest of the low," or simply "no class." Shopkeepers, publicans and skilled tradesmen occupied the premier positions, each family having its own sphere of influence. A few of these aristocrats, whilst sharing working-class culture, had aspirations. From their ranks the lower middle class, then clearly defined, drew most of its recruits—clerks and, in particular, schoolteachers (struggling hard at that time for social position). Well before translation those striving to "get on" tried to ape what they believed were "real" middle-class manners and customs. Publicans' and shopkeepers' daughters, for instance, set the fashion in clothes for a district. Some went to private commercial colleges in the city, took music lessons or perhaps studied elocution—that short cut, it was felt, to "culture"—at two shillings an hour, their new "twang," tried out later over the bar and counter, earning them a deal of covert ridicule. Top families generally stood ever on the lookout for any activity or "nice" connection which might edge them, or at least their children, into a higher social ambience. But despite all endeavor, mobility between manual workers, small tradesmen and the genuine middle class remained slight, and no one needed to wonder why; before the masses rose an economic barrier that few men could ever hope to scale. At the end of the Edwardian period an adult male industrial worker earned £75 a year; the average annual salary of a man in the middle classes proper was £340.

That wide section beyond the purely manual castes where incomes ranged between the two norms mentioned was considered by many to be no more than "jumped-up working class," not to be confused with the true order above: but the striving sought it nevertheless, if not for themselves, at least for their children. The real social divide existed between those who, in earning daily bread, dirtied hands and face and those who did not.

The less ambitious among skilled workers had aims that seldom rose above saving enough to buy the ingoing of a beer-house, open a corner shop or get a boarding house at the seaside. By entering into any business at all a man and his family grew at once in economic status, though social prestige accrued much more slowly. Fiascos were common; again and again one noticed in the district pathetic attempts to set up shops in private houses by people who possessed only a few shillings' capital and no experience. After perhaps only three weeks one saw their hopes collapse, often to the secret satisfaction of certain neighbors who, in the phrase of the times, "hated to see folk trying to get on."

On the social ladder after tradesmen and artisans came the semi-skilled workers (still a small section) in regular employment, and then the various grades of unskilled laborers. These divisions could be marked in many public houses, where workers other than craftsmen would be frozen or flatly ordered out of those rooms in which journeymen forgathered. Each part of the tavern had its status rating; indeed, "he's only a tap-room man" stood as a common slur. Nevertheless, whatever the job the known probity of a person conferred at once some social standing. "She was poor but she was honest" we sang first in praise, not derision. I remember neighbors speaking highly of an old drudge, "poor but honest," who had sought charing work with a flash publican new to the district. "I dunno," he told her, "but come tomorrer and fetch a 'character.'" She returned the next day. "Well, yer brought it?" he asked. "No," she said, "I got yours an' I won't be startin'!"

Many women and girls in the district worked in some branch of the textile industry. Of these, we accepted weavers as "top" in their class, followed by winders and drawers-in. Then came spinners. They lacked standing on several counts: first, the trade contained a strong Irish Catholic element, and wages generally were lower than in other sections. Again, because of the heat and slippery floors, women worked barefoot, dressed in little more than calico shifts. These garments, the respectable believed, induced in female spinners a certain moral carelessness. They came home, too, covered in dust and fluff; all things which combined to depress their social prestige. Women employees of dye works, however, filled the lowest bracket: their work was dirty, wet and heavy and they paid due penalty for it. Clogs and shawls were, of course, standard wear for all. The girl who first defied this tradition in one of Lancashire's largest mills remembered the "stares, skits and sneers" of fellow workers sixty years afterwards. Her parents, urgently in need of money, had put her to weaving, where earnings for girls were comparatively good. They lived, however, in one of the newer suburbs with its parlored houses and small back gardens. To be seen in such a district returning from a mill in clogs and shawl would have meant instant social demotion for the whole family. She was sent to the weaving shed wearing coat and shoes and thereby shocked a whole establishment. Here was a "forward little bitch," getting above herself. So clearly, in fact, did headwear denote class that, in Glasgow, separate clubs existed for "hat" girls and "shawl" girls. Nevertheless, before 1914 even, continued good wages in weaving and the consequent urge to bolster status had persuaded not a few to follow the lone teenager's example. By the end of the war, in the big-town cotton mills at least, coats and shoes could be worn without comment.

Unskilled workers split into plainly defined groups according to occupation, possessions and family connection, scavengers and night-soil men rating low indeed. Following these came a series of castes, some unknown and others, it seems, already withered into insignificance in Professor Hoggart's Hunslet of the 1930s: first, the casual workers of all kinds—dockers in particular (who lacked prestige through the uncertainty of their calling), then the local street sellers of coal, lamp oil, tripe, crumpets, muffins and pikelets, fruit, vegetables and small-ware. Finally came the firewood choppers, bundlers and sellers and the rag and boners, often whole families. These people for some reason ranked rock-bottom among the genuine workers. It may have been that firewood sellers rated so very low socially because they competed in some districts with small teams of paupers who went about in charge of a uniformed attendant hawking firewood, chopped and bundled at the Union. Workhouse paupers hardly registered as human beings at all. Even late in the nineteenth century ablebodied men from some Northern poorhouses worked in public with a large P stamped on the seat of their trousers. This not only humiliated the wearer but prevented his absconding to a street market where he could have exchanged his good pants for a cheap pair—with cash adjustment. The theft of "workhouse property" was a very common offense among the destitute.

Forming the base of the social pyramid we had bookies' runners, idlers, part-time beggars and petty thieves, together with all those known to have been in prison whatever might be their ostensible economic or social standing. Into this group the community lumped any harlots, odd homosexuals, kept men and brothel keepers. Hunslet's sympathy with a prostitute, mentioned in *The Uses of Literacy*, seems unusual even during the thirties. In the proletarian world of my youth, and long after, the active drab was generally condemned out of hand, certainly by "respectable" women. Their menfolk agreed or remained uneasily silent. Nor did retirement lead to social acceptance. I recall one street walker, ten years after ceasing her trade, blamelessly married, with a "clean doorstep and a beautiful house of furniture," who was still cold-shouldered by her neighbors. Drunk one day, she could stand it no longer and burst in a passion through her doorway, half pleading, half enraged. "It's not what I was!" she screamed again and again, "it's what I am now—a decent, clean-living woman." This, over a knot of startled children playing in the street, to rows of closed, condemnatory doors. The moralists found it hard to forgive and they never forgot. "I wonder," sniffed one old neighbor to another, after hearing of the outbreak of the Second World War, "I wonder if Mrs. J., with her husband away, will go on the game again, like what she did last time?"

I don't recall, though, that any "lost women" ever threw themselves off bridges in despair, as they grew older most found a complaisant male to marry or live with and dwelt, if not accepted, at least tolerated by most neighbors.

Drunkenness, rowing or fighting in the streets, except perhaps at weddings and funerals (when old scores were often paid off), Christmas or bank holidays could leave a stigma on a family already registered as "decent" for a long time afterwards. Another household, for all its clean curtains and impeccable conduct, would remain uneasily aware that its rating had slumped since Grandma died in the workhouse or Cousin Alf did time. Still another family would be scorned loudly in a drunken tiff for marrying off its daughter to some "low Mick from the Bog." With us, of course, as with many cities in the North, until the coming of the colored people Irish Roman Catholic immigrants, mostly illiterate, formed the lowest socio-economic stratum. A slum Protestant marrying into the milieu suffered a severe loss of face. Such unions seldom occurred.

At all times there were naturally many unsnobbish people in the working class who remained indifferent to the social effects of affluence or poverty on those about them and who judged others not at all by their place and possessions. On the whole, though, most families were well aware of their position within the community, and that without any explicit analyses. Many households strove by word, conduct and the acquisition of objects to enhance the family image and in so doing often overgraded themselves. Meanwhile their neighbors (acting in the same manner on their own behalf) tended to depreciate the pretensions of families around, allotting them a place in the register lower than that which, their rivals felt, connections, calling or possessions merited. In this lay much envy (envy was the besetting sin), bitterness and bad blood which, stored up and brooded over, burst on the community in drunken Saturday night brawls. Tiffs over children usually provided the opening skirmishes, but before the fighting proper began between the males, housewive's shrieked abuse at one another, interspersed with "case history" examples aiming to prove to the world that the other party and its kindred were "low class"or no class at all. One waved, for instance, a "clean" rent book (that great status symbol of the times) in the air, knowing the indicted had fallen in arrears. Now manners and morals were arraigned before a massed public tribunal; innuendos long hinted at found blatant proof, and shame fought with outraged honor screaming in the gutter: a class struggle indeed! Purse-lipped and censorious, the matriarchs surveyed the scene, soaking it all in, shocked by the vulgarity of it all, unless, of course, their own family was engaged. Then later, heads together and from evidence submitted, they made grim readjustments on the social ladder.

As a child before the First World War I hardly knew a weekend free from the sight of brawling adults and interfamily dispute. It was then one saw demonstrated how deeply many manual workers and their wives were possessed with ideas about class; with some, involvement almost reached obsession. Yet in examining the standards of the Edwardian lower orders one has always to bear in mind that street disturbers, gutter fighters and general destroyers of the peace came from a comparatively small section of the community. Nevertheless, in the "dialogue" of street dissension one saw exposed all the social inhibitions of the more respectable.

One or two proletarian authors, writing about these times and of the slump between the wars, appear to me to sentimentalize the working class: even worse, by too often depicting its cruder and more moronic members they end by caricaturing the class as a whole. In general, women in the slums were far from being foul-mouthed sluts and harridans, sitting in semi-starvation at home in between trips to the pub and pawnshop, nor were most men boors and drunken braggarts. People en masse, it is true, had little education but the discerning of the time saw abundant evidence of intelligence, shrewdness, restraint and maturity. Of course, we had low "characters" by the score, funny or revolting: so did every slum in Britain. Such types set no standards. In sobriety they knew their "place" well enough. Very many families even in our "low" district remained awesomely respectable over a lifetime. Despite poverty and appalling surroundings parents brought up their children to be decent, kindly and honorable and often lived long enough to see them occupy a higher place socially than they had ever known themselves: the greatest satisfaction of all. It is such people and their children now who deny indignantly (and I believe rightly) that the slum life of the industrial North in this century, for all its horrors, was ever so mindless and uncouth as superficial play and novel would have a later generation believe.

Position in our Edwardian community was judged not only by what one possessed but also by what one pawned. Through agreement with the local broker the back room of our corner shop served as a depot for those goods pledged by the week which owners had been unable to redeem before nine o'clock on Saturday, when the local pawnshop closed. Our service gave women waiting on drunken or late-working husbands a few hours' grace in which to redeem shoes and clothing before the Sabbath, and so maintain their social stake in the English Sunday. Towards our closing time there was always a great scurrying shopwards to get the "bundle." Housewives after washday on Monday pledged what clean clothes could be spared until weekend and returned with cash to buy food. Often they stood in the shop and thanked God that *they* were not as certain others who, having no clothes but what they stood in, had sunk low enough to pawn ashpans, hearth rugs or even the "pots off the table." Other customers tut-tutted in disgust. News of domestic distress soon got around. Inability to redeem basic goods was a sure sign of a family's approaching destitution, and credit dried up fast in local tick shops. Naturally, the gulf between those households who patronized "Uncle," even if only occasionally, and those who did not gaped wide. Some families would go hungry rather than pledge their belongings.

The interest charged on articles pawned was usually a penny in the shilling per week, one half being paid at pledging time (Monday) and the other on redemption of the goods (Saturday). Much trucking went on among neighbors, and this often led to dispute. One woman, as a favor, would make up a bundle of her clothing for another to pawn. The pledger would then gradually gear her household economy to the certainty of hocking the same bundle every Monday morning. But the boon would be withdrawn with "I don't know whose clothes they are—mine or hers!" Then came bitterness, recrimination and even a "stackup" street fight.

The great bulk of pledged goods consisted of "Sunday best" suits, boots and clean clothing. Their lying with Uncle provided not only cash but also convenient storage for households with next to no cupboards and where the word "wardrobe" was yet unknown. Among that body of "white slaves," the washerwomen, there was always one notorious for pledging the clothes she had laundered professionally. Bold with booze from the proceeds of her crime, she would then send her client (usually a publican or shopkeeper) the pawn ticket and a rude verbal message ending her contract forever. But even in those days washerwomen were hard to come by and the good one, though occasionally dishonest, could always find labor at two shillings per diem.

Behind his cold eye and tight lip our local broker, it was said, had a heart of stone. Only one customer, he boasted, had ever "bested" him. An Irish woman he knew as a "good Catholic" had presented him with a large bundle containing exactly the same washing week after week for months on end. At last he ceased to open it and paid her "on sight." Suddenly she disappeared and left the goods unredeemed. Weeks after a revolting smell from the store room forced him to open her pledge. He found, rotting gently among rags, an outsize savoy cabbage.

Few shopkeepers indeed would lend cash. Women customers at our shop very seldom asked for a loan but their husbands, banking on a wife's good name, would send children from time to time—"Can yer lend me father a shilling, an' he'll give yer one an' three at the week end?"

"Tell him this is a shop," my mother would snap, "not a loan office."

This usually happened on the day of some big race. If the would-be punter's fancy won, he blamed Mother bitterly for robbing him of his gains.

Only those in dire straits, and with a certainty of cash cover to come, patronized the local blood-sucker; he charged three-pence in the shilling per week. To be known to be in his clutches was to lose caste altogether. Women would pawn to the limit, leaving the home utterly comfortless, rather than fall to that level.

Though the senior members of a household would try to uphold its prestige in every way, children in the streets had the reprehensible habit of making friends with anyone about their own age who happened to be around, in spite of the fact that parents, ever on the watch, had already announced what company they should keep. One would be warned off certain boys altogether. Several of us, for instance, had been strictly forbidden ever to be seen consorting with a lad whose mother, known elegantly as the She Nigger, was a woman of the lowest repute. Unfortunately we could find nothing "low" in her son. A natural athlete (he modeled his conduct on Harry Wharton of the *Magnet*), a powerful whistler through his teeth, generous, unquarrelsome, Bill seemed the kind of friend any sensible lad would pick. We sought him out at every opportunity but took very good care to drop him well away from home base. He accepted our brush-off meekly, but in the end protested with a dignity which left the other three of us in the group deeply embarrassed. "Why," he asked, "won't you be seen with me in the street?"

We looked at one another: "It's—it's your old lady," I mumbled at last—"You know!"

"I can't help what the old lady does, can I?" he asked.

"It's not us," we explained lamely. "It's them—you know—them at home. . . ."

He turned and walked away.

All of us were then within a few weeks of leaving school; no longer children. We went again to our common haunts but he came no more; the friendship was over.

Through our teens we saw him pass often, but he ignored us. The break would have come in any case, I told myself uneasily. He got a job after school as a mere chain horse lad; we had become apprentices of a sort; but a social barrier had risen for good.

The class struggle, as manual workers in general knew it, was apolitical and had place entirely within their own society. They looked upon it not in any way as a war against the employers but as a perpetual series of engagements in the battle of life itself. One family might be "getting on"—two or three children out to work and the dream of early marriage days fulfilled at last. The neighbors noted it as they noted everything, with pleasure or envy. A second household would begin a slip downhill as father aged or children married. They watched, sympathetically perhaps, or with a touch of *schadenfreude.* All in all it was a struggle against the fates, and each family fought it out as best it could. Marxist "ranters" from the Hall who paid fleeting visits to our street end insisted that we, the proletariat, stood locked in titanic struggle with some wicked master class. We were battling, they told us (from a vinegar barrel borrowed from our corner shop), to cast off our chains and win a whole world. Most people passed by; a few stood to listen, but not for long: the problems of the "proletariat," they felt, had little to do with them.

Before 1914 the great majority in the lower working class were ignorant of Socialist doctrine in any form, whether "Christian" or Marxist. Generally, those who did come into contact with such ideas showed either indifference or, more often, hostility. Had they been able to read a *Times* stricture of the day, most would have agreed heartily that "Socialist is a title which carries in many minds summary and contemptuous condemnation." They would have echoed too its pained protests on the iniquities of the doctrine. "To take from the rich," said a leader in 1903, à propos a mild tax proposal, "is all very well if they are to make some more money, but to take from the rich by methods that prevent them replacing what is taken is the way to national impoverishment from which the poor, in spite of all doles and Socialist theories, will be the greatest sufferers."

Meanwhile, though the millennium for a socialist few might seem just around the corner, many gave up struggling. The suicide rate among us remained pretty high. There was Joe Kane, for instance, an unemployed laborer who was found by a neighbor blue in the face with a muffler tied about his neck. Some time previously he had taken carbolic acid and bungled that attempt too. But the magistrate didn't think much of Joe's efforts.

"If the prisoner," he said, "is anxious to go to heaven, one would have thought he could have managed it by some better means than that. He could, now, have thrown himself into the river, or something else."

The prisoner was discharged. But several months later Joe took up the magistrate's thoughtful suggestion and drowned himself in the canal.

Throughout a quarter of a century the population of our village remained generally immobile: the constant shifts of nearby country folk into industrial towns, so common during the previous century, had almost ceased; though our borough was still growing at a diminished rate. A man's work, of course, usually fixed the place where his family dwelt; but lesser factors were involved too: his links, for instance, with local kith and kin. Then again, he commonly held a certain social position at the nearby pub, modest, perhaps, but recognized, and a credit connection with the corner shop. Such relationships, once relinquished, might not easily be reestablished. All these things, together with fear of change, combined to keep poor families, if not in the same street, at least in the same neighborhood for generations. There was of course some movement in and out, and naturally we had the odd "moonlight" flitting when a whole household, to dodge its debts, would vanish overnight. Everybody laughed about it except the creditors. What newcomers we got were never the "country gorbies" whom my grandfather remembered as the "butt of the workshops" in his youth, but families on the way up or down from other slums of the city: yet new neighbors or old, all shared a common poverty.

Even with rapidly increasing literacy during the second half of the nineteenth century, years were needed, sometimes decades, before certain ideas common to the educated filtered through to the very poor. By 1900, however, those cherished principles about class, order, work, thrift and self-help, epitomized by Samuel Smiles and long taught and practiced by the Victorian bourgeoisie, had moulded the minds of even the humblest. And slow to learn, they were slow to change. Whatever new urges might have roved abroad in early Edwardian England, millions among the poor still retained the outlook and thought patterns imposed by their Victorian mentors. For them the twentieth century had not begun. Docilely they accepted a steady decline in living standards and went on wishing for nothing more than to be "respectful and respected" in the eyes of men. For them the working-class caste structure stood natural, complete and inviolate.

Suggestions for Additional Reading

"Old" Labor Historians

This volume has virtually ignored the "old" labor historians, except as they have been criticized by the "new" labor historians. This is necessary in a book on the "new" generation, but it is somewhat unfair. Some of the older generation had a broad understanding of working-class life. Foremost in this category are J. L. and B. Hammond, especially in their labor trilogy, *The Village Labourer, The Town Labourer* and *The Skilled Labourer.* Fortunately all three have recently reappeared in paperback form. Another broad, sympathetic historian was Georges Duveau in *La vie ouvière en France sous le Second Empire* (Paris, 1946) and in *1848: The Making of a Revolution,* translated by Georges Rudé (New York, 1966).

Almost all of the "old" labor histories provide a wealth of information. Some of the more helpful ones are G. D. H. Cole and Raymond Postgate, *The Common People 1746–1938* (New York, 1939); Eduard Dolléans, *Histoire du mouvement ouvrier* (Paris, 1936); Jurgen Kuczynski, *Labour Conditions in Western Europe 1820–1935* (London, 1935); Emile Levasseur, *Histoire des classes ouvrières* (Paris, 1899); Val Lorwin, *The French Labor Movement* (Cambridge, 1954); Franz Mehring, *Geschichte der deutschen Sozialdemokratie* (Berlin-Ost, 1960); E. Martin Saint-Léon, *Le Compagnonnage* (Paris, 1901); and S. and B. Webb, *The History of Trade Unionism,* new edition (London, 1911). Kuczynski also wrote a short, synthetic work which has been translated by C. T. A. Ray, and published in paperback as *The Rise of the Working Class* (New York, 1971).

"New" Labor History: Economic Activism

The three best-known historians of the new generation have all written on Luddism and other forms of early labor disputes. Mr. Thompson's contribution has been cited; Mr. Rudé's can be found in *The Crowd in History,* and Mr. Hobsbawm's in his *Labouring Men.* All rely to some extent on an earlier work, F. O. Darvall's *Popular Disturbances and Public Order in Regency England* (London, 1934). For other forms of archaic industrial protest consult the relevant chapters in Rudé, *The Crowd in the French Revolution* (Oxford, 1959), and Hobsbawm's *Primitive Rebels* (Manchester, 1959). Much more detailed studies of early, local labor movements have been done by Fernand Rude in *L'Insurrection lyonnaise de novembre 1831, Le Mouvement ouvrier à Lyon de 1827–1832* (Paris, 1967), and Maurice Agulhon in *Une ville ouvrière au temps de socialisme utopique, Toulon de 1815 à 1851* (Paris, 1970). Both works have been issued as paperbacks. Articles on early nineteenth-century strikes continue to appear in journals like the *International Review of Social History,* the *Journal of Social History* and *Le Mouvement Social.*

Although Thompson, Rudé and Hobsbawm have put most of their effort into studies of early or archaic types of economic protest, Hobsbawm has also written essays on unionization in late nineteenth-century Britain. An excerpt from one essay appears above. Another important essay deals with the gas workers union, "British Gasworkers 1873–1914," in *Labouring Men.* A more thorough if rather less inspired general work is Henry Pelling's *A History of British Trade Unionism* (Harmondsworth, 1963). Still more detailed and sophisticated is H. A. Clegg, A. Fox and A. F. Thompson, *A History of British Trade Unionism,* vol. I (Oxford, 1964). This book goes further than Hobsbawm does in placing unions in their larger industrial context. Other studies discuss British unions in their local context: S. Pollard, *History of Labour in Sheffield* (Liverpool, 1959); H. A. Turner, *Trade Union Growth, Structure and Policy* (Toronto, 1962), on Lancashire; and J. E. Williams, *The Derbyshire Miners* (London, 1962). Many of the studies of particular unions are rather uncritical, but two of the better ones include P. Bagwell, *The Railwaymen* (London, 1963); and J. Fyrth and H. Collins, *The Foundry Workers* (Manchester, 1959).

The most provocative work being done on French unions involves the revolutionary syndicalists. Here one thinks of Peter Stearns's *Revolutionary Syndicalism* (New Brunswick, 1971), which argues that the revolutionary syndicalists did not play an important role in strike activity at the turn of the century. A more traditional interpretation, which maintains that the revolutionary syndicalists were important, is F. F. Ridley's *Revolutionary Syndicalism in France* (Cambridge, 1970). Perhaps because the French unionized later and less thoroughly than the British, the French labor historians have paid less attention to unions. They have, however, dealt with conditions conducive to unionization. One particularly interesting study is Joan W. Scott's "The Glassworkers of Carmaux, 1850–1900" in S. Thernstrom and R. Sennett, eds., *Nineteenth-Century Cities* (New Haven, 1969). In this essay, Ms. Scott stresses the role of attachment to a city.

On German trade union history, consult W. Abendroth, *Die Deutschen Gewerkschaften* (Heidelberg, 1955); W. Hirsch-Weber, *Gewerkschaften und der Politik* (Köln, 1959); and H. J. Varain, *Die Freie Gewerkschaften, Sozialdemokratie und Staat* (Düsseldorf, 1956). For books in English, see the books on Social Democracy in the section on political militancy, below. More specialized studies include M. J. Koch, *Die Bergarbeiterbewegung im Ruhrgebiet zur Zeit Wilhelms II* (Düsseldorf, 1954); and H. Kral, *Streik auf den Helgen— die gewerkschaftlichen Kämpfe der Deutschen Werftarbeiter vor dem Ersten Weltkrieg* (Berlin, 1964).

Strike patterns seem to be a more attractive topic for French and German labor historians. One very long-range perspective on French (and non-French) strikes is to be found in E. Shorter and C. Tilly, "The Shape of Strikes in France, 1830–1960," *Comparative Studies in Society and History* 13 (1971). Other essays look at the effect of the business cycle on strike activity. One might be mentioned: M. Perrot, "Grèves, grévistes et conjoncture," *Le Mouvement Social,* 1968. A whole series of articles appears in D. Schneider, ed., *Zur Theorie und Praxis des Streiks* (Frankfurt a.M., 1971).

Political Militancy

Many of the works on early economic activism cited above also contain essays on early political militancy. In addition, there are two contrasting works by more conservative English historians: R. J. White, *Waterloo to Peterloo* (London, 1957); and D. Read, *Peterloo* (Manchester, 1957). Other French histories dealing with early political militancy are A. Soboul, *The Parisian Sans-Culottes and the French Revolution* (Oxford, 1964); and D. Pinkney, *The French Revolution of 1830* (Princeton, 1972).

The excerpt from Asa Briggs's *Chartist Studies* is part of an introduction to a collection of essays on Chartism in various localities. Most of the essays merit reading. So, too, does an article by D. J. Rowe on "Chartism and the Spitalfield Silk-weavers," *Economic History Review,* 1967. This is an article on why one professional group did not join in Chartist activities—a good balance to all the studies of those who did join. Chartist physical force leaders have also been the subjects of biographies: for example, A. R. Schoyen, *The Chartist Challenge: A Portrait of George Julian Harney* (New York, 1958).

To the studies of the Revolution of 1848 by Duveau and Rudé should be added R. Gossez, "Diversité des antagonismes sociaux vers le milieu du XIX⁰ siècle," *Revue économique,* I, 1956; and by the same author, *Les ouvriers de Paris* (La Roche-sur-Yon, 1967). For German workers from 1815 to 1871 see the relevant sections of T. S. Hamerow, *Restoration, Revolution, Reaction* (Princeton, 1958). A more detailed study of workers in the revolution is P. Noyes, *Organisation and Revolution* (Princeton, 1966).

From the Revolution of 1848 to the advent of the Socialist parties has been a relatively neglected period. Recently, though, R. Harrison has published six essays on English labor and politics from 1861 to 1881 called *Before the Socialists* (London, 1965); and F. Balser has published a two-volume study on *Sozaldemokratie 1848/49–1863* (Stuttgart, 1963). As well, the French have put out numerous studies of the Commune of 1871, especially during the centenary year. See the special issue of the *International Review of Social History,* 1971, devoted solely to the Commune. One of the more rigorous studies came out before the centenary: J. Rougerie, *Procès de communards* (Paris, 1964).

An exhaustive listing of recent works on Socialist parties would double the length of this book. Suffice it then to mention only some of the most helpful, namely H. Pelling and F. Bealey, *Labour and Politics* (London, 1958); A. Noland, *The Founding of the French Socialist Party* (Cambridge, 1956); K. Schorske, *German Social Democracy, 1905–1917* (New York, 1965); and G. A. Ritter, *Die Arbeiterbewegung im Wilhelminischen Reich* (Berlin, 1959).

The tendency has been to focus on workers and socialism. This makes a study by A. Silver and R. T. McKenzie on conservative workers, called *Angels in Marble* (Chicago, 1968), an almost unique contribution to our knowledge.

Working-Class Life

Reference has been made to the articles in P. A. M. Taylor's *The Industrial Revolution in Britain* (Lexington, 1970). For often-neglected comparisons see Jean L'Homme, "Le pouvoir d'achat de l'ouvrier français au cours d'un siècle: 1840–1940," *Le Mouvement Social,* no.

63, 1968; C. Jantke and D. Hilger, *Die Eigentumlosen* (Freiburg, 1965); and F. D. Marquardt, "Pauperismus in Germany during the Vormärz," *Central European History,* no. 2, 1969. The new discipline is discussed by S. Pollard in "Factory Discipline in the Industrial Revolution," *Economic History Review,* 1963; and by E. P. Thompson in "Time, Work Discipline, and Industrial Capitalism," *Past and Present,* no. 38, 1967.

To get a broader picture of working-class housing in the nineteenth century see the other articles in Chapman, *The History of Working-Class Housing,* and J. N. Tarn, *Working-Class Housing in Nineteenth-Century Britain* (New York, 1971). *Victorian Cities,* edited by Dyos and Wolff (London, 1973), contains articles on working-class ghettos and their problems.

Working-class families during the Industrial Revolution have been studied to different effect than Mr. Anderson does, by N. Smelser in *Social Change in the Industrial Revolution* (London, 1959). P. Laslett comments briefly on the post-Industrial Revolution working-class family in *The World We Have Lost* (New York, 1965). Willmott and Young have continued their work on the family and community in two other books: *The Evolution of a Community* (London, 1963), and *Family and Class in a London Suburb* (London, 1960).

Willmott and Young's books are particularly valuable because they rely heavily on the workers' own descriptions and remarks. Earlier social investigators also reproduced workers' conversations, giving us an idea of the workers' conception of themselves and their position in society. The best example of such an investigator (actually a journalist) is Henry Mayhew in *London Labour and the London Poor,* 4 volumes (Magnolia, Mass., Reprint of the 1862 edition), or in a selection by E. P. Thompson and E. Yeo entitled *The Unknown Mayhew* (New York, 1971). The number of writers on workers who were or are members of the working class is very limited. Two autobiographies and a diary might be mentioned because they are currently available: W. Andrews and J. Gutteridge, *Master and Artisan in Victorian England* (New York, 1969), and J. Benoit, *Confessions d'un prolétaire* (Paris, 1968). Writers who have risen from the working class are not much more numerous, but they are generally more literate. One beautiful example is R. Hoggart in *The Uses of Literacy* (London, 1957).

Other aspects of working-class life which have been the subject of study include immigration and criminality in L. Chevalier, *Laboring Classes and Dangerous Classes* (New York, 1973); religion in K. Inglis, *Churches and the Working Class in Victorian England* (London, 1963); temperance in B. H. Harrison, *Drink and the Victorians* (Pittsburgh, 1971); and education in J. F. C. Harrison, *Learning and Living, 1790–1960* (London, 1961).